SHATTER PROOF

How I Overcame the Shame of Losing
My Parents to Opioid Addiction
(and Found My Sideline Shimmy)

"Lauren Sisler's bold honesty and remarkable courage in sharing the heartbreaking story of her parents' tragic overdose deaths have undeniably been a part of her healing journey. Through *Shatterproof*, she extends this healing to her readers, offering them a glimpse of resilience that resonates well beyond the pages. Just like the college football stories she brings to life, Lauren's narrative leaves her audience inspired to face challenges head-on, persevere through adversity, and emerge victorious, embodying the spirit of a true champion."

 —NICK SABAN, Former Alabama Football Coach
  Seven-Time National Champion

"*Shatterproof* is a memoir with a mission. Lauren Sisler offers the unvarnished, unflinching truth about her parents' deaths from opioid addictions to help prevent others from going through the same anguish she did. Her strength and courage have inspired me, and her book will bless and equip you."

 —JOHN C. MAXWELL, Best Selling Author, Speaker, and Coach

"With courageous honesty and vulnerable candor, *Shatterproof* reveals the devastating losses that tested Lauren Sisler's faith to the breaking point. Her story demonstrates the way God meets us in our pain when we seek shelter in His Spirit and follow the example of Jesus. Inspiring us to consider the hardest parts of our own stories, *Shatterproof* breaks our hearts and then soothes us with the hope that heals."

 —CHRIS HODGES, Senior Pastor, Church of the Highlands
  Author of *Out of the Cave and Pray First*

"Lauren Sisler is further proof that champions come in all shapes and sizes. Her journey through adversity is heartbreaking. But the lessons learned, and the powerful message within, are both compelling and inspiring! Lauren reminds all of us, even in our darkest moments, there's a glimmer of light to lead us forward."

 —FRANK BEAMER, Former Virginia Tech Football Coach
  College Football Hall of Fame (2018)

"I am in awe of Lauren's strength and resilience. To defy the odds and use her own tragedy to help others is truly beautiful. No matter your situation, *Shatterproof* has wonderful advice for overcoming obstacles and discovering your best self. Don't miss Lauren's storytelling. This is a must-read!"

— LAURA RUTLEDGE, ESPN Host and Reporter

"Lauren Sisler boldly shares the tragic story of her parent's double lives. *Shatterproof* is a must-read for anyone dealing with the scars and unimaginable pain of losing a loved one to a drug addiction."

— GENE CHIZIK, National Championship Football Coach
Auburn Tigers (2010)

SHATTER PROOF

How I Overcame the Shame of Losing
My Parents to Opioid Addiction
(and Found My Sideline Shimmy)

LAUREN SISLER

HIGH BRIDGE
BOOKS & MEDIA

Printed in the United States of America
ISBN (Paperback): 978-1-954943-99-5
ISBN (Hardcover): 978-1-962802-07-9

High Bridge Books titles may be purchased in bulk for educational, business, fundraising, or sales promotional use. For information, please contact High Bridge Books via www.HighBridgeBooks.com/contact.

Published in Houston, Texas, by High Bridge Books.

For
Mom and Dad
John and Mason
Auntie Linda

Contents

1

She's Not Going to Make It

MY MOM DIED JUST BEFORE TWO O'CLOCK IN THE MORNING on Monday, March 24, 2003, while I slept peacefully in my dorm room 500 miles away. The rescue squad transported her body from our two-story brick house deep in the mountains of southwest Virginia to a nearby hospital.

Giles County's emergency services team had gotten to know our home well in the last few months. Working with incongruent information, however, the ambulance driver had gone to the wrong medical facility, so Mom's body had taken a final tour around the countryside for well over an hour after she had passed away.

Once Mom had finally been delivered to the correct location, a dispatcher received yet another phone call concerning our residence. This time, the victim was my dad.

By now, four hours and ten minutes had ticked by since Mom had died, and Deputy Eric Thwaites was speeding down the narrow, two-lane road that wound through Newport, Virginia, to our address on Boars Head Trail.

He reached our gravel driveway on the left and turned in. The car's tires crunched the gravel underneath, and its headlights shone brilliantly between the dark rows of trees on either side of the lane. When Thwaites pulled up to our house, he spotted a dim light inside one window. With no other interior or exterior illumination, the splinters of sunlight cracking over the horizon gave the scene its only real visibility.

Thwaites met fellow deputy Teddy Vaughn outside our family's house. They knocked, then opened the unlocked door and announced their presence. Stillness and silence answered them.

In the kitchen, they found my dad, Butch Sisler, lying prone on the floor. A cursory inspection told them Dad was already dead, but Vaughn called the hospital for instructions anyway. While his colleague was still on the phone, Thwaites heard the ambulance pull into the driveway. He exhaled. The EMTs would take care of Dad's body and start the search for answers to the questions the night had raised.

Privately, Thwaites held his suspicions about what was going on. A seemingly healthy couple had just passed away, with the wife's death preceding the husband's by only a few hours. Thwaites wouldn't share his speculations with Vaughn or anyone else, though. He would wait until the coroner reviewed the facts.

For now, Deputy Thwaites just had to make sure no one else was in our home and that no intruder had invaded our refuge. Using his flashlight, Thwaites inspected each room carefully. The deeper he proceeded into our house, the more he felt like he was walking through a dream. He hadn't been a Giles County sheriff's deputy for long, and he had no training or on-the-job experiences to help him understand the cold scene that now resided within the warm and inviting home.

In the family room, Thwaites opened the drapes. By now, early morning light streamed through the picture windows, and Mom's glass coffee table cut the sun's beam like a prism. The beige sofa and Dad's oversized brown recliner that bookended the coffee table both looked new. A stack of books and an array of carefully arranged decor, however, evoked the cozy, lived-in feeling Mom liked.

Olan Mills photos along with framed snapshots hanging on the walls gave every indication of a family of four who deeply loved each other. *This home is remarkably well kept*, Thwaites thought, a tribute to Mom's precise and orderly ways. This wasn't the kind of house a sheriff's deputy got sent to on a regular basis.

In my parents' master bedroom, however, Deputy Thwaites saw everything he needed to know on the bedside table. Nevertheless, he cracked the door into the bathroom where the tub still held tepid water. From there, he walked through the hallway, peeked into a small office, and then headed upstairs.

First, he checked my brother Allen's bedroom. Four deer heads looked back at him from their final resting places on the wall. NASCAR memorabilia, forest green carpet, and military gear filled the rest of the space around the well-made bed. Nothing seemed out of place.

Then, Thwaites opened the door to my room and switched on the light. An entire wall adorned with gymnastics trophies and medals confronted him. Pictures of me, first as a young girl and then as a teenager, tall with light blonde hair, were carefully arranged around the bedroom. In one photo, I stood on a podium, hands held high with a gold medal around my neck. In others, I stood smiling with my parents, coaches, or teammates.

Thwaites was right in his assessment of my love for sports—those mementos he discovered in my room were the early seeds for my work today as a sideline reporter for ESPN.

But all that was more than a decade away…

On that dreadful morning at my home in Virginia, Deputy Thwaites closed his eyes in dismay. He prayed for the girl who lived in this room—without even knowing my name—to survive this, to somehow withstand the double tragedy of losing both parents in one night.

That poor little girl with all her trophies and medals, Deputy Thwaites thought as he flipped off the light. *She's not going to make it. She'll be shattered.*

The Sisler Family (1988)   *Our home tucked in the Blue Ridge mountains of Giles County*

The medals and trophies that Deputy Thwaites saw in my room the day my parents died.

2

Landing a Place on the Team

11 Months Earlier
Saturday, April 13, 2002
Level 10 Regional Gymnastics Competition
Allentown, Pennsylvania

M Y CAREER AS A COLLEGIATE GYMNAST HUNG ON THE UN-
even bars in front of me.
If I didn't deliver the performance of my life, I was headed home.
No athletic scholarship. No college gymnastics team. No four-year degree
for me. Even if I could learn to be content with community college, Mom
and Dad wouldn't be.

I looked across the gym. Chrystal Chollet-Norton, head gymnastics
coach at Rutgers, sat behind the judges' table. She was the one I had to impress. To her right stood an entire wall of bleachers. That was the spectator
area where Mom and Dad sat.

Standing on the floor next to the chalk box, with leather grips on my
hands, hair trimmed neatly, wearing a black velvet long-sleeve leotard
with rhinestones, I watched the gymnasts in front of me complete their routines. Gymnastics had been my life for 14 of my 17 years, so although I still
liked watching other gymnasts, I knew how to lock in and stay focused.
While I did mental reps over and over in my head, other female athletes
cleared bars nearly eight feet off the floor. My turn was coming.

I chalked up, tightened my grips, and then stepped up next to the mat
and continued to visualize my bar routine in my mind. After each mental
rep, I would run in place to keep my circulation up and my anxieties down.

As I kept my blood pumping, my eyes drifted around the room, observing all the taped ankles and wrists. I took notice of my own body, remembering the injuries that had almost erased my career before it had even begun.

My parents always believed in my dream, but they were realists, too. After my injuries two years earlier, Dad had sat me down for a talk. "Lauren, you don't have to do this. If the pain is too much, you can quit. We will support you in that decision."

I knew he meant it. My parents were proud of my athletic accomplishments, but they didn't believe in letting aspirations overwhelm good sense. Nothing Dad said had changed my mind. No pain, no matter how severe, could make me bail on my ambitions.

Instead of letting my injuries take me out, I used them to motivate my victories. In a sport that has one of the highest injury rates among female athletes, I'd been through my share of pain. It was my dream to one day serve other athletes as a sports medicine physician.

That is why I'd put everything I had into getting recruited for a collegiate team. It wasn't just that college gymnastics was as close as I would ever get to the Olympics or that it was an aspiration I'd held for nearly a decade—landing a spot on a team would also solve the college question for my family.

Mom and Dad's recent financial problems made it impossible for them to cover my impending college tuition, and the cost of medical school was out of the question.

At first, we'd believed the Air Force Academy was my ticket to higher education. We were a military family, and the U.S. armed services were our heritage. Dad was a veteran, and I had even been born on the U.S. Naval Base in Guantanamo Bay, Cuba, when he was stationed there. My older brother, Allen, followed in his patriotic footsteps and also joined the Navy. In fact, while I was soaring on the bars, Allen was inspecting survival gear and rigging parachutes. Dad was flying high with pride.

For a while, we thought I had the Academy locked up. Their gymnastics coach had been actively recruiting me for their team, and I loved the idea of leaving my sleepy small town for the high life of the Colorado Rockies.

Everything was shaping up perfectly according to my plan for my life.

Then my SAT scores changed the game. They didn't clear the bar for the Air Force Academy. I took the SAT three times, but with each attempt, my scores dropped lower. That made three tries and no wins. Even I knew when I was defeated.

Once Air Force Academy was off the table, I followed up with other schools of interest that had received my recruiting video—West Virginia University, the University of North Carolina, and North Carolina State University. All were close to home, each an excellent school for both academics and athletics.

Due to my injuries, though, my videos were out of date. Coaches wanted something more recent. They even called my house and asked what I had done lately. The honest answer was "Nothing much because I've been injured," which is never a great answer if you want an athletic scholarship. Only walk-on offers came through—no scholarships attached.

My only hope lay with Rutgers, which still had one unoffered scholarship spot left on their team. I was either going to wow Chrystal Chollet-Norton in the next five minutes or watch my parents' and my dream slip from my grasp after we'd hung on for nearly 14 years.

I say dream, but it was more like a lifetime investment. The countless practices, competitions, sweaty loads of laundry, extra reps in the backyard, hours in the gym, gallons of gas in the car, pep talks before meets, and planning for the future all led to this moment. It wasn't just me on those bars.

All my family's hard work and hope had landed on this one event.

BANG! A loud noise jolted me from my thoughts.

The young gymnast competing ahead of me lost her grip and fell from the high bar. She didn't hop right up like the polished athlete she was, so I knew something was wrong. When she finally moved, I saw her elbow. It was the most gruesome injury I had ever witnessed in all my years of gymnastics. People ran to her from all sides of the gym.

I tried to stay warm and keep myself composed, but the traumatic scene unfolding in front of me was shaking my focus. The longer the emergency on the mat dragged on, the more my rhythm was thrown off. My palms began to sweat, and I pictured myself falling from the bars, breaking my bones, and shattering my hopes for the future.

Lisa Mason, my club coach, came up to me at the chalk box, put her hands on my shoulders, and looked me in the eye. "Focus, Lauren," she said. "You got this. Just focus."

I steadied my breathing and centered my thoughts around my next event. I didn't want to callous myself to the sad incident in front of me, but

I could do nothing for the girl on the mat. If her pain affected me, we would both lose.

Pain is the price of admission to life—and to competitive gymnastics.

It seemed like forever until the medical team got the injured girl moved off the floor safely, and it was my turn to perform. *Go big, Lauren,* I told myself. *Going home is not an option.*

Just before I saluted the judges, I caught a glimpse of Mom and Dad watching me from the bleachers, where they had been for nearly every competition I'd entered since I was five years old.

This is for us. All of us.

I mounted the bars and swung into action.

With each successful turn around the bar, my odds of going to college and becoming a doctor increased, but I couldn't think about the next 10 years. All I could do was focus on the next turn, the next hand placement, the next breath.

I hit each skill in the routine, and I knew it was good—better than good. It was the best I had ever performed, and all I had left was the dismount. I swung my legs and flew around the bar faster and faster, gaining the momentum I needed for the big release.

I let go of the bar and tucked my body as all my dreams spun in the air around me. All of my parents' effort and money and all of my focus for the last 14 years culminated in those seconds.

My feet hit the ground, and my hands flew above me.

I stuck the landing, saluted Coach Chollet-Norton, and practically flew off that mat. I looked to the bleachers and saw my parents screaming and clapping with unrestrained joy. As soon as I finished the meet, I ran to where they were sitting. We threw our arms around each other and hugged and danced and cried right there in front of whoever was watching.

I babbled something to them, but I don't think anything I said made much sense. I was a 17-year-old bundle of nerves, sweat, and tears, but my parents understood me. I could feel their arms around me, and their pride in my work seeped into me.

"Lauren?"

I heard my name behind me.

It was Chrystal Chollet-Norton.

I let go of my dad and mom to turn around. "Yes?"

"I'd like to offer you a scholarship and a spot on the Rutgers gymnastics team. Are you ready to be a Scarlet Knight?"

Chrystal Chollet-Norton held out her hand. I grabbed it. "Yes I am!" I told her without an ounce of hesitation. "Well then," she said. "Welcome to Rutgers."

Level 10 gymnast alongside teammate Kearstin Myers

*With Mom and Dad at my Level 10 gymnastics banquet
just before graduating from high school in 2002*

3

A New Computer and Collateral

Summer, 2002
Giles County, Virginia

WHEN MOM AND DAD GOT HOME AND STARTED MAKING plans for me to leave for college, they realized there was a little more to that "Welcome" that wasn't said out loud.

What Chrystal Chollet-Norton really meant to say was, "Welcome to Rutgers, if you can pay the rest of the tuition that the gymnastics scholarship doesn't cover." And my parents could not. Right that minute, they couldn't afford to pay the power company.

How, Mom sometimes wondered, *did two educated, middle-class, church-going Americans end up in this shape?* She couldn't understand it, and frankly, neither could anyone else who knew our family.

For months, Mom had been writing $10 checks to each of the utility companies in lieu of paying the bills in full. She hoped her token gesture would keep the lights, water, and gas turned on. So far, it had. And so far, she had successfully kept me in the dark about their financial freefall.

What mortified her, though, was having to go to her family with her hand out. Mom adored her parents, Edwin and Jeannette Dornbush, her brother Ross, and especially her sister, Linda. Growing up, Mom had been the lively sibling who delighted her dad and saved her allowance to take her mother out to lunch. My aunt Linda had been the responsible sibling who tried to keep everyone on track. Despite their different lives and personalities, Mom and Linda always turned to each other for support and friendship.

Mom had despised asking her sister for the money to get my prom dress out of layaway, but she hadn't exactly had a lot of choice in the matter. The money wasn't there, their credit was maxed, and Mom wasn't about to let me miss my senior prom. As Mom asked, Aunt Linda kept their deal a secret from me, so I never knew it wasn't Mom's money that paid for my formal attire.

It wasn't just the occasional big expense Mom needed help with. For the past two years, her dad had paid our mortgage — at least, Mom told him his contributions were paying for the mortgage. She probably didn't want to think about Gramps' reaction if he knew the truth.

For that matter, Mom herself could hardly bear to think about the truth. The person she was becoming wasn't the person she knew she was deep inside. The change bothered her, and she wondered if other people noticed.

I suspect my mom didn't even know if the starry-eyed young lovers who met on a blind date at Jumbo's Pizza & Subs in Roanoke would even recognize the older versions of themselves. She and Dad were once so in love, so innocent, spending all their time writing love letters to each other while Dad was away at boot camp. After so many years of loving hard and working harder, it seemed like their lives were unraveling, slowly at first, and then more aggressively so that they were now left threadbare.

A longtime wife and mom, my mother had never pursued a career that would bring in the dollars. She had earned a degree from a community college and worked as an administrative assistant for a short time when we kids were younger, but what she really felt called to do was be a mom and provide for her family at the house. So she devoted her time and energy to helping us kids be successful and picked up work where she could.

Mom was already paying for my gymnastics tuition by working in the back office at the gym. Of course, I had no idea she was doing anything other than offering some of her time to help with filing while I tumbled through my four-hour practice sessions. And as long as Mom and Dad had anything to say about it, I never knew more than that.

Dad also did what he could for the family, but it never seemed to be enough. Despite a solid career in bio-engineering, my father's financial situation had deteriorated rapidly. He had already depleted his retirement accounts, and he owed the Salem Veterans Administration Medical Center where he worked for all the extra personal time he had taken. Plus, he and

Mom had borrowed everything they could get from my aunt Linda and uncle Mike Rorrer.

Mom started every new request for money with the same phrase: "I'll pay you back." My aunt knew her sister sincerely meant to pay her back, but somehow things had gotten way out of hand, and no money ever appeared. The situation clearly bothered Mom, which meant it bothered Linda too.

Finally, Aunt Linda sat Mom down. "I know you want to pay me back, Lesley. But I also see you can't pay right now, so let's not bring it up every time we talk. I'd rather focus on something more positive." It seemed to Linda that Mom felt better after their chat, which made her feel better, too.

Even though Linda supported Mom as much as she could, she voiced her concerns over her sister's choices and struggles. In fact, Linda had tried to introduce a different perspective, hoping it would help her sister get a handle on her family's financial life.

"Why does Lauren have to go Rutgers anyway?" Aunt Linda had wanted to know. "Lauren is a great gymnast, but if you can't pay, then you can't play."

Mom didn't look at it that way. My brother Allen and I were her life, and she would make sure we had the best she could obtain for us.

"Couldn't Lauren go to a state school, then?" Linda asked when I wasn't around to eavesdrop. "Maybe live at home? Do gymnastics for fun instead of competing on a collegiate team?"

Mom gave a cold shoulder to any suggestion that involved downsizing my career or education. However, she continued to rely on her sister for financial assistance.

Chrystal Chollet-Norton's scholarship offer covered just $9,000 of Rutgers' $24,000 out-of-state tuition. Other financial aid took care of a few thousand more, and Dad and Mom signed a Parent PLUS loan to help cover the $8,000 balance. In their situation, what was another $8,000 in debt? Broke was broke.

But not even the loan was the last straw. No, the last straw, the cherry on our family's seven-tier financial cake of debt was the computer.

I couldn't show up at Rutgers without a desktop for my dorm room. Maybe Mike and Linda would spring for that, Dad suggested when I was out of earshot. There was no harm in asking, Mom agreed.

As it turns out, there was harm in asking. Mike and Linda had already forked over so much money that the request for more irritated my normally patient uncle. "You put Lauren at Rutgers on a partial gymnastics scholarship," Uncle Mike pointed out when Dad made his pitch for the loan. "Tuition is $24,000 a year, and she's getting $9,000. Do the math. You can't even cover her tuition, so you sure can't buy her a computer!"

Dad turned on the charm, emphasizing that the money was for my education, and Uncle Mike finally caved as Dad had suspected that he would. "I'll cover the computer, and then you pay me back on a monthly plan," Mike said as he handed over his credit card … again.

When Dad returned from the computer store with a top-of-the-line Dell desktop along with a printer and a package of ink cartridges, poor Uncle Mike hit the roof. "This is the last straw," he told his brother-in-law. "I want that money back."

You can't wring blood from a stone, though, and Dad knew it. He borrowed $100 from my grandma and used it to cover part of the computer loan. While I swung obliviously on the high bars, Dad was riding a merry-go-round of debt, each transaction making him go faster in a circle and getting him nowhere. Years later, I still think he really believed he would be able to hop off at some point.

In addition to the cash, Dad turned over his collection of antique Japanese ginsu knives and rare coins. He had spent years browsing through antique stores and gun shows, and the collection was the only thing of value Dad could lay his hands on at a moment's notice.

Uncle Mike did not share my father's interest in collectibles or understand why he valued antiques. "What is all this stuff?"

"Collateral," Dad said.

Uncle Mike had no choice but to accept it.

After storing the knives and coins in my aunt and uncle's house, Dad went outside and promptly asked Aunt Linda for $50 to put gas in the car. As usual, she handed over what Dad asked for.

Close-knit though we were, the family was growing annoyed with all of Dad and Mom's requests for aid, and they certainly didn't understand why a father who had worked his whole life and had minimal living expenses couldn't fill up the car with gas. Understand or not, though, the family was still helping out. More importantly, they weren't asking any questions. That was good.

Mom and Dad didn't want to answer any.

Dornbush family photo
(from left to right: Ross, Linda,
Jeannette, Edwin, Mom)

Mom with Aunt Linda, not just
sisters but best of friends

The courthouse in Millington,
Tennessee, where my parents got
married in 1981 when my dad
was stationed there in the Navy

A sweet treasure I found along with
all the letters my dad wrote to my
mom while he was away at boot camp.
I admire the love they shared for
one another.

4

Rutgers, At Last

Thursday, August 29, 2002
Giles County, Virginia

THE BIG DAY FINALLY ARRIVED. MY PARENTS AND I LOADED UP their Mercury Sable station wagon for the trip to New Jersey. Freshmen couldn't have a car on campus, so I had to leave my beloved teal Pontiac in Virginia.

Mom, ever organized and attentive, had assembled everything and labeled it with my name — just in case I might lose a box somewhere between the parking lot and my dorm room. Even my shower shoes had a label!

We didn't have enough room for everything I had packed, so we borrowed my coach Lisa's car carrier, strapped it to the roof, and filled it with more belongings. I was prepared for whatever life might throw at me.

The three of us drove me along with all my worldly possessions, including the now-infamous Dell desktop, all the way from Newport to Rutgers. Mom and Dad moved my stuff into my dorm, Clothier Hall, and they met my roommate, Kara Spector—whom I loved and adored the first time I saw her.

Mom helped me spread some of my favorite mementos around my room. We put my new computer—purchased with Rorrer money—on my desk and added a sign that read "With God, all things are possible." I loved the metallic scriptwriting and the cool black background. To protect the walls in Rutgers' hallowed halls of learning, I used sticky tack to hang a copy of my favorite poem, "Footprints in the Sand." It's the one that ends with the lines:

"I don't understand why, when I needed
You the most, You would leave me."
He whispered, "My precious child,
I love you and will never leave you
Never, ever, during your trials and testings.
When you saw only one set of footprints,
It was then that I carried you."

Before every single gymnastics meet, I would read that poem out loud as a reminder that God was there by my side, walking beside me each day and ready to carry me when life's greatest challenges would arise.

Even today, I can see the look of sheer joy on my parents' faces when they helped me unpack that last box. As we said our goodbyes and my parents walked out that door, I knew they were proud of their little girl.

And as for me, well...

Look out New Jersey! I was 17 years old and ready to be independent.

Let me be clear. I was as independent as Coach Chollet-Norton, a competitive gymnastics team, a bunch of demanding professors, and fun-loving Kara would let me be. In other words, I was busy!

College proved to be everything I hoped for. Coach Collet-Norton challenged my athletic skills in new ways. The academically demanding coursework kept me studying diligently for the grades I needed to gain med school admission, and Kara was always there, making sure I had a good time. And be assured that we had a *great* time!

"You're amazing, Laur," Kara told me more than once. "You can go to a party, dance for five straight hours, have more fun than anybody else there, and never drink a drop."

Kara was right. I *could* dance longer than anyone else, and I *couldn't* stand alcohol. It just never appealed to me. Maybe that was the way I was wired. My mom drank a beer every now and then but nothing more than that.

Or maybe I didn't imbibe because I had seen my dad drink a little too much more than once. He would go on a weekend bender a few times a year when I was a kid, and I hated the way alcohol changed him. After a few too many drinks, my dad would move from laid back and fun-loving to "ornery."

When he was drinking, I would insist that my friends and I play at their houses instead of them coming over to my house the way they usually did. What if they noticed something was "off" at the Sislers' place?

When my dad drank, it also created a lot of tension between him and Mom. He would have to ask off from work because of a hangover, or in a drunken stupor, he would make irrational purchases that further set back my parents.

I hated when it happened, but his occasional binging never got in the way of our relationship. It would happen, I would try to keep to myself, he would sleep it off, and after a couple days, things would go back to normal.

After each binge, Dad regretted it. He didn't like drinking. Mom didn't like him drinking. So I didn't drink. My parents didn't have to tell me to avoid drugs, either, but I could have easily gotten my hands on some if I had wanted them.

In the early 2000s, drugs had already penetrated deeply into rural America. By the time I graduated from Giles High School, a small single-A school that runs the coveted single-wing offense in football, drugs had already infiltrated every social group. I'd seen kids getting high on the weirdest stuff by the ballfield at the town park or in the parking lot after a football game. Some of my high school peers took to pills, marijuana, and a new drug called fentanyl, but I steered clear of all that.

The drug scene at Rutgers was slicker and more overt than it was in Giles County. One time, I walked into a room at a frat party and saw three guys doing lines of coke. I was mortified and hurried into another space before anyone could see me.

Clearly, I was not naïve to drugs and alcohol. I just thought life was too exciting and held too much promise to squander it on substance abuse.

Besides, Kara and I knew how to have real fun. We hooked up an old-school Nintendo to a small TV in our room and went nuts on that thing. We LOVED playing Nintendo, mostly Tetris and Tecmo Bowl.

We did the classic roommate activities like watching movies together and making ice cream runs, but we also created our own fun. One time, when it snowed a deep New Jersey snow, Kara and I went to the dining hall and got meal trays to use as sleds. We laughed and formed a strong bond in ways unrelated to partying.

In fact, Kara later shared with me that she was so homesick when she got to Rutgers that she at first thought about leaving school and going back home. But she told me that because of our friendship and the fun memories we created together, she changed her mind, found happiness, and decided she was meant to be there at Rutgers.

And it wasn't just Kara and I having fun. Lots of other people hung out in our room, too. Life was as good as it had ever been—or as it ever would be again.

Even though I filled nearly all my time with fun and dancing, I still made time for my family. Mom, Dad, and I set up a regular communication calendar and decided we would talk on the phone every day. Sometimes, I would page my dad at his job at the VA medical center just to talk to him. If I thought my mom would be home to answer the phone, I'd call her there. When I could, I'd wait until after seven o'clock to call because I knew they'd both be at the house, and we could all three get on the call at the same time.

In 2002, cell phones were still pretty new, and my parents didn't have one. I did, but I didn't have an unlimited minute plan.

The cell phone was actually a big surprise. Soon after I moved to Rutgers, Grandma and Aunt Linda came to New Jersey with Uncle Mike when he was taking his medical board exams at a hotel near the university. Mom had sent a credit card with Aunt Linda along with orders to get me a new cell phone. Oddly enough, the card had my name printed on the front of it.

With my shiny, new credit card in hand, I went shopping at a nearby Verizon store with Grandma and Aunt Linda. I was more reasonable about technology than cars, so I picked out a simple phone and calling plan. It turned out that I could not have even purchased a burger for dinner let alone a cell phone—there was no credit with that card. The store would not accept it, so Aunt Linda had to call Mom and work something out. It was decided that Grandma would buy the phone and make the monthly payments, and Mom would pay her back. I sent the card back to Mom.

The cell phone was a real blessing to me. No matter when I called, or even how often, Mom always wanted to hear about my progress in gymnastics. Dad … well, he just wanted to hear my voice. It felt good to know that I was still Daddy's girl even if I was now a flourishing pre-med student and collegiate athlete at a prominent New Jersey school.

As much fun as I was having at Rutgers, I couldn't wait to go home for Thanksgiving and see my family again. We had made so many memories together over the years. Gosh, I loved my parents.

Move-in day at Rutgers in 2002   *Freshman dorm Clothier Hall*

My roommate, Kara, and me. My, oh my, how much
changes from freshman year to senior year!

The first photo I took with the Rutgers gymnastics team
as a freshman. I'm in the back row, fourth from the left.

5

A Scrapbook of Sweet Memories

Childhood
Roanoke, Virginia

I TURNED 10 ON THE 10TH DAY OF THE 10TH MONTH OF THE YEAR. I was 10 on 10/10. Pretty cool, huh?

It only seemed right that I'd get an especially big gift for such an important birthday. I knew that my parents had to count their pennies sometimes though, so I wasn't sure what I would get for my present that year.

Nothing special was there when I went to bed, and that worried me a little. But when I woke up, a full-size trampoline sat in my backyard! I don't know how my parents got that thing put together in the middle of the night. Maybe they had help. Maybe Santa has birthday elves who work the non-holiday shift. Whatever the story, I had my very own trampoline, and I was beyond thrilled!

I choreographed what I envisioned to be my future college floor routine when I imagined I would be a world-famous gymnast. I danced to Frankie Valli and the Four Seasons or the *Dirty Dancing* soundtrack. Even as a kid, I loved the top oldies and classic rock hits.

That trampoline was the best gift I'd ever received.

Soon, my parents started buying me other gymnastics equipment. First, it was a balance beam with a tumbling mat and then a set of bars. With these things, I could practice at home and not just in the gym. My parents went above and beyond to give me what I needed not only to perform well but to exceed expectations, competition after competition.

I loved those afternoons and weekends when I could practice my routines to the scent of fresh-cut grass. My parents often worked in the yard while I showed off my new skills. I wanted them to see my best, and they wanted to give me the best.

While our family never cracked the code for becoming wealthy, gifts were definitely my dad's love language. One Christmas, Allen and I got bikes.

We had wanted them so badly. We told our parents that we just *had to have them*. When we got up that Christmas morning though, no bikes sat under the tree. Instead, we had a note from Santa, which read, "Sorry, kids. I wasn't able to get the bikes this year. They wouldn't fit on my sleigh. Maybe next year."

At first, I felt bitterly disappointed, but Allen, older and wiser than I, kept prodding Dad about them. Pretty soon, our morning turned into a scavenger hunt. We found another note from Santa hidden in the limbs of the Christmas tree, and we scurried from our spots by the bay window where the small gifts sat to search the rest of the house.

At one point, we were scouring the perimeter of the house, front and back yards. We made our way to the basement and looked around the entire garage. Finally, tucked away in one of the back storage rooms, we found those shiny new bikes with big bows tied around the handlebars.

Allen was dancing around like, "I knew it; I knew it all along. I knew the bikes were down here!" And I was just excited, screaming with joy as I jumped on mine, checking out all the bells and whistles of my brand-new ride.

Does it sound like my parents spoiled us rotten? I guess you could say they did. They got us everything we wanted, but fortunately, what we wanted was never over the top. Mostly, we just wanted to have fun and be together.

Mom had mastered the art of celebration.

She specialized in holidays. Mom always found a way to contact the Easter Bunny and have him bring a basket with exactly the right selection of goodies and treats for Allen and me. Somehow, that bunny always managed to sneak out before we could catch him.

Each Christmas, all four of us decorated the house. We draped lights outside, and then we'd all go together to pick out a tree. Mom loved decorating the tree. It was Allen's and Dad's job to festoon it with lights, and then Mom and I would add the decorations.

Mom also loved baking Nanny's jam-filled butter cookies, which were Gramps' favorite. On holidays, my grandma Sisler, whom I always call MawMaw, Grandma and Gramps, and Aunt Linda and her sons, Justin and Jason, would often come over. I also cherish fond memories with my mom's brother, Ross Dornbush, my Aunt Becky, and four cousins, Jonathan, Benji, Luke, and Hannah.

Several other relatives would pile in the house, too, and without fail, my mom would cook every single person's favorite food, snack, or dessert, and our table groaned under everything from peanut butter fudge to corn pudding. She loved entertaining the family while we kids ran through the house, playing hide and seek.

Every year, Gramps shot footage of us on his big RCA CPR300 camcorder. I still have the home videos he recorded. My favorite one shows me in my nightgown, sitting on Dad's lap as Gramps goes around the room asking everyone in the family to say Merry Christmas while Bing Crosby croons *White Christmas* in the background. In the video, I'm wriggling with excitement because it's Christmas Eve and Santa is on his way.

Mom didn't just celebrate the big holidays though. Better than anyone else I've ever known, my mom understood the importance of honoring life's everyday milestones. All the years I was a competitive gymnast, Mom kept a scrapbook. Every award, card, or note from a coach was tucked in that scrapbook. Mom also added to it herself. She loved going to the Hallmark store and buying credit-card-sized notes with Bible verses or inspirational sayings printed on them.

Before every single gymnastics meet, Mom would write me a card, complete with her own handwriting and one of those little Hallmark inspirational quotes. Over the years, I collected so many of these that Mom bought baseball card sleeves to store them in.

I can still see myself sitting on the bed of a hotel in Virginia Beach where we'd gone for me to compete, that scrapbook open in my lap. Mom and Dad sat on either side of me. After reading every one of those cards aloud to them, I told them that "Footprints" was my favorite.

As supportive as Mom and Dad were, they didn't fight my battles for me. I see a lot of sports parents make that mistake. These parents get so used to being an advocate for their kids that they don't stand back and let the kids learn from their mistakes. Mom and Dad weren't like that. They let me learn, and I discovered that sometimes, learning hurts. Like the time I smarted off to my coach Lisa as a bratty teenager—that one hurt. They didn't run interference for me or defend my actions. I had to own my inappropriate behavior, call Lisa, and apologize myself.

My parents got it right where others fail.

Every single night I was home until the day I left for Rutgers Mom and Dad tucked me into bed. We said prayers and read Bible verses or inspiring stories together before I drifted off to sleep. Even as a kid, I knew that when I grew up, I would be a mom just like my mom. My future husband would be a dad just like my dad. And our kids would never have to worry about anything because we would take care of them—just like my parents always took care of me.

When I was in elementary school, MawMaw offered our family a chance to live in her house in Roanoke while she stayed with my great-uncle on his farm. Mom and Dad appreciated the opportunity to save money on housing, so MawMaw moved out. Her house in Roanoke was a ranch-style home with all the living space on the main level and a basement below. I was a kid, so I liked anywhere we lived as long as we were all together.

My parents weren't city people though, especially my dad. He didn't want to live in Roanoke forever, or even a day longer than he had to. Mom and Dad dreamed of living as far out in the country as they could go. They envisioned decorating and then hosting family functions in a mid-size two-story brick house located in the heart of the Blue Ridge Mountains. They wanted to see the stars when they looked up at night.

Maybe because Mom and Dad loved rural America so much, I grew up going to what we called "the farm" a lot. The farm was actually a spread of several hundred acres in Giles County that belonged to my great-uncle Allen, the man my brother is named after. Uncle Allen raised cattle in open pastures.

On the farm, we could ride three-wheelers across the open country. A small creek ran along the property, and we loved to play there, too. Often, we would pitch a tent, build a fire, and camp out for a night or two at a time—just me, Allen, Mom, and Dad.

It could have been the farm's cozy atmosphere that called their names, or maybe it was just something born in them, but for some reason, my parents decided that we couldn't keep living in town any longer, even though the rent was free and the location was convenient. Consequently, we moved out of MawMaw's house in 1998, when I was in the eighth grade.

Mom and Dad had acquired five acres of Uncle Allen's property in the remotest part of Giles County, and they designed a three-bedroom, three-bathroom home just for us. They called it their "dream home." They would have to stretch to meet the mortgage, but the dream beckoned, and my parents followed. Between gymnastics, the military, and now a two-story brick home, we Sislers were about as all-American as apple pie.

My parents might have been better dreamers than planners, however. They were so anxious to get to the country that we left MawMaw's house before our new home was move-in ready. In the interim, Mom and Dad moved us into the tiniest, ugliest mobile home I had ever seen—the infamous pea-green trailer! I didn't even let my friends visit me when we lived there. (It would have been fun if I had, though, since my parents had started letting me stay by myself sometimes while they were out.)

Once when I was alone in the trailer, I tried to make one of those styrofoam cups of noodles for a snack. It looked easy when Mom did it. Without reading the directions, I peeled off the container's top and stuck the whole thing in the microwave. I punched in the time and pressed start.

In about a minute, flames shot out of the microwave. Apparently, you need to add water if you want to make microwave noodles.

The air smelled like I'd tried to burn the whole place down, so there was no hiding what I'd done when my mom got home, but I shouldn't have worried. I didn't get in trouble—I almost never did.

Mom simply laughed at me and shook her head. "Next time," she said, "read the directions."

Next time, read the directions. Here ends one of Lesley Sisler's best lessons in cookery. My mom was a wonderful cook. Her sausage gravy and her chili were family favorites. When I had time to spend at home, I loved being with her in the kitchen.

I didn't spend much time on cooking or household chores, though. Mom made sure I did my homework and worked hard at gymnastics practice before anything else. She and Dad took care of all practical matters, and they organized everything when we moved to the new house.

Ironically, after we left it, that awful trailer was donated to the fire department where they set it ablaze, and firefighters in training practiced putting out flames. I sure could have used their help when we lived there!

At 12 years old, I didn't know enough to appreciate what I had in the pea-green fire trap. All I saw was my shoebox of a room and the hideous paint on the trailer's metal exterior. Looking back, however, I see Thanksgiving. I see four people seated in front of a hot turkey dinner served on folding tray tables in the den. I see a football game on TV afterward. I see Washington defeating Dallas. I see a family being a family.

What wouldn't I give if—right this minute—I could go back to that trailer for just one more meal? I wouldn't care if it was a Thanksgiving dinner with all the trimmings or a cup of scorched noodles.

Speaking of food, Dad loved Chinese food.

I've inherited his love for Asian cuisine. If I'm going to visit a relative's house, I might even stop by a Chinese restaurant to grab an order before I get there.

When I was a kid, though, Dad's Chinese food obsession—and my mom's desire to save money—got me in trouble.

I was about nine years old when Mom and Dad took me to the local Asian buffet. I say, "Took me." Really, they left me outside. They did it for good reason—the restaurant would make them buy a third to-go container if they saw me—but I didn't like being made to wait in the car. So I didn't. I went dashing into the restaurant where Dad was filling up the takeout containers and Mom was paying.

"Didn't we tell you to sit in the car?" Mom asked.

Obviously, they had. And just as obviously, I hadn't obeyed.

"You're not listening very well today," Dad said, and then he added those famous words nearly every kid has heard: "You're grounded."

It was the first time—and as it turned out, the only time—my dad ever grounded me. I don't think my grounding went quite the way Dad expected. At that point in my life, I wasn't accustomed to receiving a punishment of any kind, and I didn't take it lying down.

When we got home with the Chinese food, my brother made everything worse by raiding Dad's tool chest without permission. Allen and his friends were building a big fort out in the woods nearby, and they needed some of Dad's tools for their construction project.

For that little adventure, Dad scolded Allen, who in turn vented his frustration by hitting the garage door. Or rather, he meant to hit the garage door. In fact, he missed the door completely and put his fist right through the window. The broken glass sliced his wrist open. Dad grounded Allen first, and then we took him to the ER to get him stitched up.

After we left the hospital with Allen and an antibiotic prescription for his stitched-up wrist, I kept bugging Dad the whole way home about being grounded. "It just isn't fair!" I said.

"You know what? I'm sick of listening to you," Dad finally said. "I don't want you in my hair anymore. Go put on your bathing suit, and we'll go to the pool."

My grounding had lasted about three hours—most of which I spent whining to my dad at the ER—and it ended with a trip to the pool where I met up with my best friend, Ellie Augustine. Allen ended the day up at the tree fort with the tools.

Dad was better at handing out gifts than he was at dispensing discipline. For him, love was big-hearted. It knew no walls, had no thresholds, and respected no boundaries. As it turned out, love without boundaries would be the downfall of our family.

*Mom, Dad, and me
before I could walk*

*Dad carrying me through the park
near our home in Roanoke*

Learning to walk with Mom

*Dad loved coaching Allen in
Little League Baseball.*

Doing a handstand on the balance beam in my backyard when I was about 10 years old. The famous trampoline sits in the background.

After the trampoline and balance beam, my parents added the bars to my backyard setup.

My childhood best friend, Ellie Augustine, and me when we were nine years old

Mom snapped this photo as Allen and
I ripped open our Christmas presents.

The last Christmas at home with my family
before graduating high school

The infamous pea-green trailer that I nearly caught on fire

6

We're Still Going to Disney World!

Childhood
Southwest Virginia

SPORTS RUN THROUGH MY BLOOD, NOT ONLY AS AN ATHLETE but also as a spectator, someone always anxiously watching from the sidelines. When a game was on, I cozied up next to my mother and father in the living room in front of the TV.

Our family loved college football, and all four of us were Virginia Tech Hokies fans, but in the NFL, we pulled for Washington. Dad loved sports, but he missed a lot when we watched a game. As soon as he sat down to watch TV, he'd fall asleep. Often, he even slept with the remote control in his hand, pointing at the television like he was changing channels.

We didn't just watch sports on TV, though. We also went to see ball games and car races. My family spent a lot of time at the New River Valley Speedway where my brother was a pit crew member for a local race car driver named Rodney "Six Pack" Cundiff. We knew it was Allen's crew when we spotted Six Pack's Ford Thunderbird with a "09" painted on the side.

In 1999, when Allen was a rising senior, Six Pack's team won the first two races of the season after he transitioned from the Thunderbird to the Taurus. Allen was ecstatic!

Dad was a racecar fan, so Allen came by his love for racing honestly. He started working at the speedway when he was 16 and continued until he turned 22, even helping out on weekends when he had time off from the Navy.

Mom, Dad, and I would set up our lawn chairs on the tiered cement slabs between turn four and the finish line to watch his team race. Allen always knew where to look when he wanted to catch Mom or Dad's eye. When Allen's race divisions came up, we would cheer him on.

Of course, foodie that I am, I had to start the night off with a bag of the Little Caesar's breadsticks that they sold at the racetrack, always to be followed by a funnel cake with extra powdered sugar.

As a kid, going to the racetrack was one of my favorite things to do. Sometimes, we would even travel to the NASCAR races. Martinsville hosted a big one, and a few times, we went to the Charlotte Motor Speedway, a three-hour drive from our house. That's probably where my love of sports really took off.

When sports weren't interfering with our regularly scheduled family programming, we all four sat down to eat dinner together. My mom was a great cook, but I was a picky eater in my single-digit years. Mom's traditional, hearty meals didn't satisfy my taste buds, which had been honed on racetrack food. So she often fixed SpaghettiOs (with a dash of sugar) and mac-n-cheese for me.

Not to be outdone in the kitchen, Dad made an incredible batch of nuclear cheese dip, a recipe he had perfected while he was in the Navy.

If my mom didn't cook, we would hit up Western Sizzlin'—a family favorite. That's where Dad taught Allen and me to say, "Yes, sir," and "Yes, ma'am." Dad made sure we learned it, too! If we didn't say "sir" or "ma'am" to our server, Dad would quickly correct us and say, "Yes, *what?!*" He would keep doing that until we would say it. Dad always wanted us to use our manners and show respect toward others.

I recall that time in my life—watching sports and hanging out with my parents—as the good ol' days, a magical era when everything seemed just perfect, exactly as it should be. Now, I don't want to sound like all we did was eat cheese dip and lie around watching sports on TV. Mom and Dad made sure we played sports, too.

For my brother, almost every day meant baseball, basketball, or football practice, and for me, after-school hours filled up with gymnastics. You could usually find my dad on the sidelines coaching my brother. Meanwhile, my mom would be taking me to and from my practices and keeping tabs on my progress. She had plenty of opportunities to cheer me on. Gymnastics was my life.

I enrolled at the Roanoke Academy of Gymnastics when I was three years old. My athletic career took off quickly, and then it rocketed upward, thanks to my coaches, Barb Jirka and Lisa Mason. They saw my potential and pushed me through the levels at a quick clip. I began competing at age five. By the time I turned 10, I had reached Level 10, which meant I was competing just under the Elite Program. It's the highest level in the sport, and only a very small percentage of gymnasts ever reach it.

Prodigy comes at a price, though. Even as an elementary schooler, I trained at the gym for as many as 20 hours per week. If I wasn't in the gym practicing, I was out in the backyard practicing. Most of my time at home was spent choreographing routines and doing mental reps. As I grew up, my gymnastics career accelerated its already meteoric rise. Before long, they were calling me a "star."

My early success as a gymnast is particularly significant when you consider that I was basically a normal kid. I wasn't homeschooled. I didn't go off to a major Olympic training camp like other young athletes who show world-class performance potential. I was just fearless, and I had my family and coaches to support my dream.

That was another reason the coaches pushed me so hard. I was ready to do anything, and that attitude landed me a spot on the national stage from a young age. At 10 years old, I entered my first national competition. It was held at the Grenelefe Resort in Haines City, Florida, located right outside Orlando. Back then, the resort would flip its biggest ballroom, fill it with gymnastics equipment, and hold national meets in there.

For a budding gymnast, this meet was the event of the year. Some nights, I couldn't sleep because I was too excited about the meet, and Mom and Dad shared in my excitement. They decided to turn my gymnastics meet into a family road trip—11 hours of music, snacks, and lots of potty breaks.

Most of my memories from the trip are of the four of us jamming out to the Traveling Wilburys in the car. Occasionally, my brother would put in his own music, or I would listen to Frankie Valli and the Four Seasons on my Walkman. I loved his songs, especially "Walk Like a Man" and "Big Girls Don't Cry."

We snacked a lot on road trips. Dad was a Coca-Cola and peanuts kind of guy. He dumped the whole package of nuts in his drink. Mom ate Nabs, and Allen chowed down on beef jerky and Mountain Dew. I, on the other hand, kept a candy stash—a lockbox full of chocolate. I adored candy so much that I would alphabetize it in rows in the box. I even inventoried the candy so I would know if anyone tried to break in and steal it. Mom allowed my munching, but she told me to be moderate about it since I had a gymnastics meet.

On the way, we stopped at Daytona Beach, which I thought was cool because, unlike most shore destinations, you could actually drive on the sand. We'd driven all through the night, so the four of us watched the sunrise together over the Atlantic Ocean.

My parents scheduled most of our theme park experiences for after the gymnastics meet. As Mom put it, "We aren't getting sunburned before you compete." But because it didn't involve tons of rides and miles of walking, we decided that SeaWorld might be a good idea.

I wore Aqua Socks that day because I just knew my feet were going to get wet and I would spoil my shoes. I may have saved my shoes, but boy did my feet pay the price! I got awful blisters on both feet. Mom freaked out when she saw them. She was sure the blisters would affect my performance, the reason behind the massive road trip. Seeing as how I couldn't unblister my feet, we had no choice but to go on to the competition and hope for the best.

When I walked in and saw gymnasts milling around everywhere, my competitive nature kicked in, and I determined that I would medal in the all-around and beat the other girls, blistered feet or no blistered feet.

A gymnastics meet consists of four events: vault, uneven bars, balance beam, and floor exercise. I hit my floor routine, giving me such confidence to start the competition. Even though my feet were on fire, it went great. I moved on to bars where I had another terrific performance for someone so young. Even vaulting, which was never my strong point, went well and earned me a high score.

By this point, I had a shot—a real shot—at medaling in the all-around. All that stood between me and the podium was a solid performance on the balance beam.

The event was nearly over, and I only had to demonstrate one more skill before the dismount. All the judges wanted was a full turn on the balance beam, one of the easiest skills in the whole code of points for gymnastics. I went to do the turn, but I lost my balance and wobbled. Instead of staying upright and squaring my hips, I fell flat on my butt. I knew when I hit the mat that I'd lost my chance at a medal.

The disappointment cut deep. I'd wanted so badly to make my coaches and parents proud. We had spent all this money and time, and I'd failed because of a stinking full turn. Tears in my eyes, I started to get up off the mat. Suddenly—over the noise of the competition—I heard my mom's voice yell out: "Don't worry, Lauren. We're still going to Disney World!"

And we did!

When I transitioned from middle school into high school, I really started to push forward toward the gymnastics scholarship. My dream of competing as a college athlete kept me going even when the pain of multiple back and ankle injuries threatened my future.

Through all of the ice packs, doctor's appointments, and ibuprofen, I never hung it up. No matter the struggle, the frustration, the blood, the sweat, the tears—the pain didn't stop me. I remained unshattered.

Through the years—and the tears—I developed a close relationship with my coach, Lisa. She challenged me to be better, and her challenges felt a lot like tough love at times. That was okay with me. I responded well to tough coaching. Every time I stepped up to take my turn at a competition, I remember hearing Lisa screaming, "Lauren, you can do this. You can do this!"

Her confidence fueled me even when my courage failed.

Everyone knows that gymnastics is an extremely physical sport. To perform flips and handsprings on a balance beam and launch your body into the air off a vault requires a degree of athleticism few people attain. But there's another side of gymnastics that is just as daunting.

It takes psychological fortitude to convince yourself to perform those flips and vaults, and it requires even more mental toughness to do so in front of a crowd of people who are sitting on the edge of their seats, waiting to see if you'll crash and burn.

Coach Lisa pushed me past my edge physically and mentally, and she gave me the confidence I needed to conquer any fears and to perform— even excel—under pressure. Looking back, I see the tenacity that gymnastics built in me. Even though performing at such an intense level took it out of me at times, I'm thankful for the way it prepared me for my future.

Learning those traits, both physical and mental, was a daily practice for 14 years, but sometimes, I wouldn't go for the skills my coaches wanted me to learn. I would balk. When I just couldn't seem to stick the landing, and I was ready to be done for the day, Lisa wouldn't let up. She was always there, pushing, pushing, and pushing at first, but eventually clapping, hugging, and praising. When I'd finally mastered something tough, she was the first to congratulate me big. Having that support system in the gym was huge for me. But even Lisa's approval couldn't match the value of my parents' praise.

I always felt an adrenaline boost when I'd be training, look out through the three-foot by three-foot glass window by the gym door, and see them pop in. Even though I concentrated on my skills, I would know when they were watching me.

Some kids get embarrassed by their parents but not me. I loved having Mom and Dad around. I would think, *Oh, my parents are here! I can't wait to show them what I'm working on. I can't wait to impress them.*

Nothing felt better than nailing a new skill at practice while my parents watched, but most of the time, they wouldn't be at the gym to see it. While in most kids' sports, parents might stick around to watch practice, competitive gymnastics is a little different. I trained for four hours at a time, so my parents couldn't sit at the gym for that long, but they came as often as they could. Even when I got my driver's license and could take myself to practice, my mom would stop by to do some accounting work in the back office.

Over time, Mom came more and more often. She took on additional office work at the gym. The gym's owners were so impressed with my mom's work they even offered her a full-time job, but for some reason, she felt like that was beyond her. My mom appreciated the chance to earn extra income, but her priority was being there for Allen and me when we got home from school.

At the time, I just assumed she enjoyed the chance to do some work and hang out with the coaches, athletes, and parents. That she might have another reason for working at the gym never occurred to me, so I never asked her why she was in the gym office so frequently. Would it have made any difference in the end if I had asked?

My coaches from Roanoke Academy of Gymnastics
Lisa Mason and Barb Jirka
(then and now)

When I was six years old and my gymnastics aspirations really began to take off

Dad was always proud of my accomplishments, like this gold medal, even if he never fully understood the technical aspects of gymnastics like Mom did.

*Gymnastics portrait from 1998
(Finally, I got braces to take care of those buck teeth!)*

7

Muscle Cars and Back Injuries

Teenage Years
Southwest Virginia

AFTER WE MOVED TO OUR HOUSE IN THE COUNTRY, I GOT OUT of school early, right after the sixth period. My last class was excused for gymnastics.

"Man, you're so lucky to get out of school early," other kids would say to me. They were wrong. I wasn't getting out of school for extracurriculars or to go have fun—although gymnastics was fun. It felt more like I was going to work.

Until I got my driver's license, Mom would pick me up at school, and in the back of the car, she'd have a blue hard case thermos cooler. I'd open it up, and inside, Mom would have packed a hot meal for me to eat on the way to practice.

Mom and Dad rejoiced the day I got my driver's license and could drive myself from school to gymnastics. Of course, having a driver's license isn't enough to drive on. You need a car. And at 16 years old, I knew just the kind of car I needed—a black Mercury Cougar. I'd even seen the car on a lot in Roanoke near my dad's work, all souped up with chrome wheels and a spoiler.

Dad loved muscle cars, too. Mom was less sure. "Maybe," I told her, "I could get a Trans Am instead."

Somehow that idea didn't fly either. I didn't understand. Aunt Linda's sons, Justin and Jason, loved foreign cars, and they drove fast, tricked-out vehicles that turned heads when they sped by. Even Allen got a Ford Bronco and then a jacked-up blue F150. Why shouldn't I have a cool car, too?

Since luxury cars were out of the picture, I wound up driving my grandmother's teal Pontiac Grand Prix. It was my inheritance after Maw-Maw passed away. While the teal Pontiac might not have been the sleek Cougar of my dreams, that car was perfect for high school! Since it wasn't a pricey new ride, my friends and I had the freedom to wage (mostly) harmless vandal wars against each other's cars. It didn't matter too much if the *Gymtaz-mobile*, as I called it, got a small scratch or bump every so often.

Trista Dooley, Chelsea Keating, Mary Stafford, and Joyelle Vinson were my ride or dies. We would load up in the Gymtaz-mobile, roll down the windows, crank up the music, and spend hours riding around our small town. I can't tell you how many times we would drive through one particular neighborhood near the high school just so we could "jump the bump." I would step on the gas, topping 40 miles per hour, just before blowing through an intersection. The car would soar through the air, leaving us girls belly-laughing and sparks flying when the car finally hit the pavement.

The teal Pontiac also became my dining room. On my way to practice after my early release, I would stop to grab something to eat or chow down on the meal Mom would sometimes pack for me.

While eating in the car was no problem, homework was a no-go. Anytime I tried to read or write in a moving vehicle, I would get carsick. Homework had to wait until after gymnastics, which made for a very long night. My life consisted of school, gymnastics, homework after nine p.m., and then bed. Does it seem like a grind? It was, but in the repetition of my life, I also developed my sense of dedication.

While I was forming my own habits and driving myself everywhere, I knew MawMaw's Pontiac couldn't last forever.

One day, Dad came up the driveway in a big, hooptie car, a 1986 Mercury Grand Marquis. He climbed out and said, "Well, Lauren, I got your new ride."

I was devastated! "Where's my Trans Am?" I asked him.

Dad laughed at his own joke. He had bought that old car to get himself back and forth to work because it would save on gas. Funnily enough, I started driving it to high school a lot. Those cheap rides came back in style, and you could say I was pretty trendy. I'd stick an adapter tape into the tape deck, hook it up to my Sony Discman, and blast whatever music I was into at the time.

Mom preferred that Allen and I drive to school instead of riding the bus—another difference of opinion between her and Aunt Linda. My aunt couldn't understand why Mom and Dad would spend money on cars when they were struggling financially, but Mom wouldn't hear any of her arguments. Mom said her kids weren't riding the bus because it took 45 minutes, and driving cut it down to 25. "Besides," she added, "how else could Lauren drive herself to gymnastics practice after school?"

Through it all, Mom stood by my side. She knew everything there was to know about gymnastics. Mom followed every dismount, every landing, and every tenth of a point. She attended every event, and over time, became an expert in the sport of gymnastics.

When she asked with a big smile, "How was practice?" I never answered with just "good" or "bad." I gave details! No matter if the score was low or high, we would go out for ice cream at The Country Store or TCBY afterward. It might be a reward for a job well done, or it might be a way to help cheer me up after a discouraging performance. Either way, my mom was my biggest cheerleader.

Even though she would score me like one of the judges, Mom never pressured me like some of the other parents. I saw how that approach paralyzed my teammates who went through it, but things weren't like that with us.

While Mom became a judge in her own right, my dad learned to be a filmmaker. He borrowed my grandpa's big, old-school RCA camcorder, the kind you had to carry on your shoulder. He took it with us to every gymnastics meet.

I still have every video he made. As a sports reporter today, I laugh at his efforts at low-key broadcast journalism. Dad would put on a fake, overly professional voice and say, "Okay, here goes Lauren Sisler on the bars." I'd actually be on the balance beam. It was funny because Dad obviously knew what a good routine was. He knew when I'd stuck a landing and when I hadn't. But he never tried to be an expert. He just showed up and cheered.

Have I made it obvious yet that I was—and am—a real Daddy's girl? I mean, Mom and I were close, but when I wanted something, I knew which of my parents to appeal to.

Daddy, can Ellie come spend the night tonight?

Ask your Mom, Lauren.

No, I'd say, *you ask her for me.*

He would ask, and the answer would always be *Yes!*

Of course, at times, I took advantage of his generous spirit, but mostly, I just cherished our relationship. I remember holding his hand and taking a sleigh ride together in the winter. I remember being four years old, skipping down the street by his side.

I wish I could bring my parents into my world now. I wish Mom would call to tell me she had caught me reporting a game on ESPN. I wish Dad would get on the phone and sing our special song. He loved classic rock, and he would switch up the words to Led Zeppelin's song "Over the Hills and Far Away."

Dad would sing, "Little Lady, you got the love I need. Maybe more than enough. Oh darling, darling, darling; walk a while with me."

And I signed my notes back to him the same way: *Your Little Lady, Lauren.*

Oh, Dad, I wish you could sing that song to me and switch up the words. I wish you could walk a while with me just one more time.

With my dedication to gymnastics and my family's relentless support, I moved up the ranks quickly.

As it turned out, maybe a little too quickly.

I sustained multiple injuries, and eventually, I was sidelined. My first big injury began when I was 12 years old. Sharp pains started shooting down my legs when I would train. My mom took me to see Dr. Brent Johnson, an orthopedic doctor, to help manage the pain. Dr. Johnson diagnosed a bulging disc in my L4-5 and sent me to physical therapy.

"One more thing, Lauren," Dr. Johnson told me before we got up to leave his office. "I want you to take Aleve."

My mom nearly had a come-apart. She thought he said, "A leave," like "a leave of absence from the sport." Mom informed him I was in the middle of competition season and there was no way I could take time off. In some ways, gymnastics was her career as much as it was mine.

After the doctor reassured her that he only wanted me to take medicine for my pain, my mom cooled down, and we made our way home with a painful diagnosis and a bottle of pills.

The physical therapy—and the Aleve—helped, but my back issues continued into high school. In fact, I dealt with that pain for the rest of my athletic career, and to this day, it flares up occasionally. (Aleve still helps.)

Along with helping me manage my pain, my mom also assisted in the collegiate recruiting process. She would stuff envelopes with the best highlights from my competitions, and I would write my name, email address (gymtaz1sis@netscape.net), and phone number across the blank white label. As we sat together and stuffed each envelope, dozens of them, we felt our chances were still pretty good to land an offer. My mom's pride in me created a warm glow around our table, and I had even more peace and confidence knowing my parents had my back.

If only they could have fixed my back, our chances would have been better. While the pain of my injuries was tough, the indirect results of my injuries were excruciating. I hated not being able to do what I did best, and the injuries threatened my future as they delayed the recruiting process.

After we would send out a VHS tape of me that was a little outdated to a prospective college, they would ask for something newer, which I didn't have since my injuries kept me from competing for a stint.

Rejection letter after rejection letter appeared in our mailbox. Most of the time, the message was tempered with, "We don't have a scholarship offer for you, but we can bring you on as a walk-on." For me, that wasn't good enough. I needed the money a scholarship would bring. I couldn't go to college without it.

The biggest rejection—and probably the most painful—came from NC State. I really wanted to go there, but they only offered me a walk-on spot. The Air Force Academy, my other top choice, would have been an automatic full ride, but I didn't get accepted. The Academy wanted to send me to prep school for a year, but I didn't think it was right to put my college gymnastics career on hold. Besides, I harbored secret doubts about whether the military lifestyle was for me. I wanted to experience "real college" ... should a real college ever offer me a spot on their team.

My chances were growing slimmer, however. On top of the injuries, I hit an unusual growth spurt in my late teens. On average, female gymnasts top out around five feet. Not me. When I graduated high school, I had already hit five feet seven inches. In the following years, I gained another two inches. Women rarely continue growing at that age, but I was never one to settle for average in anything. By my late teens, I was far too tall and too lanky to meet the typical gymnast's profile.

But I had dedicated my life to the sport, and I knew the big payoff was within reach.

Despite all the rejection and physical pain, the application process was a lot of fun, and I enjoyed getting to travel to different schools and, as I saw it, be part of something pretty spectacular. I'll admit that having such a high profile as an athlete was really cool. I got to compete, stand on the podium, and even earn the gold medal at Nationals. Yes, I was a national champion a few times!

Those medals and trophies mattered a lot to me, as evidenced in my introduction to my recruiting tape where I stood right in front of my trophy display and said, "Hi, my name is Lauren Sisler. These are all my medals and trophies." Today when I watch that tape, I cringe. What felt like confidence at the time now seems like unbridled arrogance, but we've all been 16 before, right?

And for teenage me, those medals and trophies really were the anchor of my house and validation of all my accomplishments, of my entire family's sacrifices. I thought the medals would lead me through doors of opportunity. At 16, I thought the world was waiting for me. I thought I had it all.

Maybe I did.

Teal Pontiac Grand Prix,
i.e., Gymtaz-mobile

Mercury Grand Marquis, i.e., The Hooptie

AAU National Bar Champion in 1998

Giles High School graduation in 2002

8

Party at the Sislers' House!

Teenage Years
Giles County, Virginia

OUR FAMILY FASHIONED MANY MEMORIES ON THAT RURAL acreage Uncle Allen gave Mom and Dad.

For my dad, who liked peace and solitude, it was a perfect setup. My mom, on the other hand, liked to be visible in the community. She enjoyed socializing with neighbors, the people at church, and the other gymnastics parents. Later, when she and my dad began to withdraw from community life, I should have taken note. It was a sign—one of many—and I missed it.

During my high school days, though, Mom was still all about having my friends over, and of course, my friends loved going so far out in the country on weekends. My house became the "cool" house. Allen and I would invite five or ten friends up, and the next thing you'd know, half the school would be in our backyard. We would have 50 cars in the driveway before the night was over. That's the advantage of living on the side of a mountain and off the beaten path.

Of course, you can't have half a high school in your backyard at night without alcohol bottles getting passed around. My parents loved my friends, but they knew no teenager was a saint. I think Mom and Dad pieced it together that some of my friends smoked pot, but they didn't see it happening out in the open at the house.

You could catch the occasional skunk-like whiff of marijuana, and cigarette smoke hung in the air often. No overt drug use could be witnessed, but I knew that some people did partake on occasion. At a small school in a small town, there are no secrets. Your business is everybody else's business, too.

The alcohol, on the other hand, was very visible inside and outside the house. To show my friends what used to happen in the Navy, my dad once spiked a watermelon with tequila. Of course, everyone thought he was so cool for doing that.

Mom always worried about alcohol and possible substance use. To help prevent underage drinking and driving, she had people drop their keys in a little basket on the kitchen counter. Mom didn't mind the extra work to keep wayward high schoolers off the roads and out of trouble. A house full of partying high schoolers was actually a bright light for my mom who sometimes grew lonely with us living way out in the country the way we did.

What's funny about these parties in hindsight is that they would get out of hand even with my parents there. Too many people would show up with too much alcohol. The cops never got called, but I do remember waking up in the morning to the sound of beer bottles clinking together as my friends cleaned up the house.

They always woke up early to gather the trash from last night. "We've got to get this cleaned up before your parents wake up," they'd tell me. I loved that my friends respected my parents enough to do that for them.

After she got up, Mom would make breakfast, complete with her famous sausage gravy, for everyone who was still there. Being a mom was her one lifelong ambition. Those weekends, it seemed like she got to be a mom to 100 high schoolers, and no one could have loved it more.

Over time, the parties got more and more out of hand. Allen and I would sometimes have them without my parents even knowing, or I would tell Mom "just a few friends" were coming over when I knew good and well 30 people were heading for a backyard bonfire at our house.

Mom finally put her foot down. "We're not doing that again. If someone gets in an accident—if something bad happens—we'd never be able to forgive ourselves."

I begged. I pleaded. I kept inviting people over. Dad even took my side. Wouldn't she rather the kids come over and drink at our house than be out drinking somewhere else?

"Butch, what happens if they drive away under the influence and get in an accident?"

Neither Dad nor I had an answer ready for her.

In spite of my parents' fears and their repeated promises to stop the parties, the good times continued until shortly before I left home. The final straw came when a kid took out my brother's four-wheeler and wrecked it. Thank goodness he didn't end up paralyzed, but he was pretty bruised and banged up. At that point, my parents declared the bonfire bashes were over.

But Mom and Dad still had a lot of trust in me. Most of my time was spent going to and from gymnastics practices, so I didn't get to have a whole lot of social activity. Sometimes on the weekends, though, I would go to parties at other places after our high school football games. When those were over, I'd crash at a friend's home nearby rather than face the drunk drivers who might be swerving on the winding country roads between town and our house.

Mom and Dad trusted me because they knew I didn't drink, and I always stayed in touch with them about where I was. I can't say I always respected their curfew, though. I definitely pressed my luck on that a few times.

"I can't sleep when you're out," Dad would say. "Be home by midnight."

Sometimes, it would be 12:30 before I'd start up the gravel driveway to my house. Of course, you can't sneak up a gravel drive, especially not with a hyperattentive German Shepherd waiting for you.

Saber, the latest in a line of Sisler family German Shepherds, would announce my arrival to everyone who missed the crunch of the car on the gravel. I'd think, *Dang it, you're blowing my cover, Saber.*

It didn't matter if I arrived home at 10 p.m. or 1:00 a.m.; Dad was never in bed. I always found him on the couch. Sometimes he'd be sitting up wide awake, but often he would have fallen asleep waiting for me. Dad just couldn't go to bed until he was confident that his daughter had made it home safely—even though he had nothing to worry about from me.

My favorite trick was to run around the car after I parked and start rummaging through the back of it like I was looking for something. When my dad opened the door, I'd yell, "Oh, I just left something in the car. I came back to get it."

I said it so it sounded like I'd been in the house the whole time. I hadn't been, of course, and Dad knew I hadn't. He never said anything about it, though. He was cool like that.

Saber died my senior year. Dad buried him in the woods, just beyond our backyard. At that point, it was my second experience with loss, the first being my MawMaw's passing. Saber's death hit me hard.

It's shocking the way my understanding of grief would grow to new magnitudes just a year later.

9

The Last Thanksgiving Together

Wednesday, November 27, 2002
Giles County, Virginia

T HANKSGIVING BREAK ROLLED AROUND. I PULLED OUT OF NEW Jersey on Wednesday as soon as my last class was over. I couldn't wait to see my parents!

My brother got permission to leave Norfolk, where he was stationed, and come home that Thanksgiving with a Navy buddy he called "Slover." I'm forever grateful that he did.

My cousin Justin, who was like another brother to me, said he was also coming over. He would spend Wednesday night at our house and stay over Thursday for Thanksgiving dinner. Allen planned to go deer hunting on Thursday while I'd visit with Justin and help Mom pull together the meal.

It was going to be a fabulous, if short, vacation!

Sure enough, Mom rolled out the red carpet for me, stocking the house with all my favorite snacks, and Dad hugged me until I could barely breathe. It felt good to hear them call me "Woe," my nickname since childhood. Justin came as he had promised.

After dinner, Dad fell asleep in his recliner in front of the TV in the living room—the way he'd done many times before. The remote rested in his hand and pointed at the TV as if he were still watching. Allen and Slover also hit the hay early so they could get up to hunt. Mom kept her usual middle-aged bedtime of 10 o'clock.

Justin and I stayed up chatting until after midnight when I told him I was too tired to sit up anymore, and we each turned in. This was the first time back in my bed since August, and I thought it was shaping up to be a cozy holiday with my family.

I was wrong.

Thursday, November 28, 2002
Thanksgiving Day, 7:43 a.m.
Giles County, Virginia

Mom's scream woke us all out of a dead sleep.

Justin, yanked out of a dream, yelled, "Was someone shot?"

Allen, Justin, Slover, and I dashed out of our rooms, and we nearly collided at the top of the stairs. I caught a glimpse of the stricken look on Allen's face before he and Slover leaped down the steps in front of me. Mom's uninterrupted screaming sent us all into panic mode.

In the living room, Allen pulled Dad off the couch and onto the floor then rolled him onto his side but not before I saw that his face had turned blue. Blue as could be. The same shade of blue that you turn when you're not alive. I ran to his side and saw that he was taking breaths—about one every 30 seconds—each sounding like a heavy snore.

"Call 911!" Allen yelled. "And get me a spoon!" Mom, now completely panicked, was hardly able to move. Slover dashed into the kitchen. I grabbed the cordless phone and dialed it.

"911. What is the emergency?"

"This is Lauren Sisler," I heard myself saying. "I need someone out here right away. *Right away!*"

"What's going on?"

"My dad's not breathing. We need help now."

"Where do you live?"

I gasped, trying to catch my breath so I could talk. "I live on Boars Head Trail in Newport. It's about five miles down Spruce Run. On the left, there is a long gravel driveway, about a quarter of a mile. Our house is up that drive. Please hurry!"

While I gave the emergency operator our address, Slover came back into the living room with a wooden spoon. Allen used it to pry open Dad's clenched jaw. Then he twisted it to help keep the airway unobstructed. We didn't really know what to do, but it seemed like a smart move, and it must have been because Dad went from taking a breath every 30 seconds to taking one every 15 seconds.

It felt like an eternity before the EMTs burst into our house and started giving my dad professional medical attention. I later learned that it took just 17 minutes for them to get to our remote location.

Dad remained unresponsive, but they said he was breathing at a rate of about three to four times every 60 seconds. His heart rate was recorded at 115 beats per minute, but they couldn't obtain blood pressure for him. The EMTs noted a Glasgow Coma Scale (GCS) score of three, which I later discovered was the same as the GCS of a dead person.

One of the EMTs directed a piece of plastic into Dad's mouth to keep his tongue out of the way—a more sophisticated version of Allen's efforts to open Dad's airways with the wooden spoon. Twice, the EMTs attempted to insert a breathing tube, but they failed both times. In the end, they opted for bag-mask ventilation.

Another of the EMTs quizzed Mom about Dad's health and his medications. She finally calmed down enough to provide a complete answer. Yes, Mom told him, Dad had a history of cardiac problems. He was taking blood pressure medicine, a muscle relaxer, and something for mild depression.

"Was that the only medication Mr. Sisler took last night?" The EMT looked at Mom hard when he asked.

That was all, Mom assured him. She picked up Dad's John Deere coffee mug from the glass-topped table and swirled the cold remains of his drink around the cup's sides. Half an hour later, the EMTs loaded Dad into the ambulance to transport him to the hospital. When they left, Dad was alive but still unresponsive. Mom rode with him in the ambulance.

She might have calmed down, but my panic had not subsided since her scream woke me from my dreams and turned my house into a nightmare. What if Dad didn't make it? What if we got to the hospital and found out he was gone? I couldn't live without him. No way.

Since we were all too jittery to be behind the wheel, I'm still not sure who drove us to the hospital. In fact, I don't remember anything until Justin and I were standing outside the medical center.

If it comes right down to it, I don't even remember that. But we have a picture—why anybody would take a picture on that day, I don't know. It's a snapshot of Justin and me, both wearing stocking caps as it was brisk outside. Look closely at the figures in the photo, and you'll see my eyes are bright red from hours of crying.

I guess I got a head start that day on the new reality of mind-numbing grief that life was about to send my way.

At the hospital, Justin called his mom, my aunt Linda Rorrer, with the news that Dad was at Montgomery Regional Hospital. Aunt Linda said she was on her way. We clustered together in the waiting room. Mom hardly uttered a word while we waited for my aunt to arrive. Maybe she didn't feel much like talking. I certainly didn't.

Aunt Linda, however, was not in the same quiet mood we were. She arrived with an army of questions for Mom. Her first question sat at the top of all our minds: "Lesley, what's going on here?"

"I don't know yet," Mom told her before disappearing into Dad's hospital room. The hospital only allowed her and Allen in the room. After they had been there for some time, a nurse who was an acquaintance of Aunt Linda's finally emerged with a piece of real news.

"Butch is a very lucky man," he told us. "It's incredible he's even still alive."

"Really?" Linda asked. "Was it his heart condition that caused this?"

"No," the nurse replied. "It was his medications."

I let that piece of information fly right over my head and asked the one question that really mattered to me: "Can he come home?"

"He'll need to go to St. Albans for a few days. He needs further evaluations."

"He's had a lot of heart problems," I blurted out. Aunt Linda and the nurse looked at each other curiously. Then, the nurse smiled pleasantly at me, turned, and walked down the hall. Clearly, he and my aunt knew something I didn't, but it must not have been anything important.

I felt so relieved. Dad was alive. He had not had a heart attack or a stroke, just a mix-up with his cardiac medications. Thank goodness I was going to be a doctor, huh? I could make sure this didn't happen anymore.

I turned to Justin and began a conversation. It was some time before Mom returned from Dad's room.

"Let's go home," Mom said when she reached us. "We still have Thanksgiving to celebrate."

Aunt Linda glanced at her sharply. "We're having Thanksgiving? Just like that?"

"I've already fixed most of the food. Besides, Butch is fine. Nothing happened here." Mom slung her purse over her shoulder.

We all stared at her in shock.

She looked back at us and repeated her words clearly and distinctly: "Nothing happened."

Aunt Linda drove my mom and me back to our house. Justin, Slover, and Allen came separately. At home, the six of us, along with other family members, sat down at the table and consumed a full turkey dinner with all the trimmings. We ate just like Dad hadn't collapsed and nearly died in the next room a few hours earlier.

Our entire family carried on with the day as if what Mom said was true—that nothing had happened.

As it turned out, Mom was wrong. Something had happened. Something very big had happened; she just couldn't bear to have us find out about it. But denial comes with a hefty price tag.

Mom shouldn't have worried. We were all about to find out what she was hiding anyway, whether she wanted us to or not.

Oh, Mom, would anything have been different if you'd just told us the truth that day?

*Outside Montgomery Regional Hospital with
my cousin, Justin, after Dad was hospitalized on
Thanksgiving Day. (It still strikes me as strange
that we would take this photo after the day's events.)*

10

It Did What It Said It Would Do

Thursday, November 28, 2002
Thanksgiving Day, later that afternoon
Giles County, Virginia

AFTER THANKSGIVING DINNER, MOM DROVE AUNT LINDA AND my grandparents to St. Albans with clothes for Dad. The four of them joined Dad and the doctors in a conference room. Months later, Aunt Linda relayed to me what occurred there.

Gramps asked the question everyone wanted to know. "What in the world is going on?"

"I read about it," Dad replied. "It did what it said it would do."

"What are you talking about?" Aunt Linda asked in complete exasperation. "What's this 'it' you're telling us about?"

Neither Mom nor Dad replied for a long time. Finally, Dad looked at Mom and said, "Maybe you'd be better off without me."

No matter how unsatisfactory it was, that was the only answer Aunt Linda got. Neither Mom nor Dad said anything more.

For more than a year, Aunt Linda had been growing increasingly suspicious about our family's situation. Her sister, my mom, was a wonderful mother, always full of big plans and ambitions for us kids. Allen would be a Navy SEAL, Mom assured her family, and they would all see me on ESPN one day.

Despite her obvious devotion to her children—and Aunt Linda knew that my mom was an exemplary wife and mother—something wasn't right.

Aunt Linda couldn't quite put her finger on exactly when the trouble had started, but she had sensed things had been upside-down for a long time. In 1996, Mom had gone to the doctor for neck pain. It turned out to be a displaced disc. Eventually, she'd developed bone spurs, arthritis, and carpal tunnel syndrome. Everything had been okay before those medical problems began.

After each new surgery or treatment, Mom would feel better for months or even years. Then, the pain would worsen, and MRIs would show new negative developments in her spinal column. As Mom's physical problems mounted, so did her requests for money.

Dad, too, had grown increasingly erratic. Aunt Linda had suspicions about him from the start of his relationship with Mom, but she kept those concerns to herself. Mom was too poised, too carefully put together, and altogether too lovely to be involved in anything seriously wrong—wasn't she? If Dad had dug himself into a truly troubling hole, Aunt Linda hoped Mom had not gotten involved, too.

Just a year earlier, though, the sky had fallen in.

On September 11, 2001, Aunt Linda's concerns had mushroomed. Uncle Mike, an ER doctor, was slated to attend a medical conference in Florida. Aunt Linda invited Mom to come along; they could spend time at the beach or go shopping together while Uncle Mike sat in his classes.

Allen was home on leave, staying with a friend, but Mom had jumped at the opportunity to get out of rural Virginia. The three of them—Aunt Linda, Mom, and Uncle Mike—had set out for the airport around seven in the morning. Mom had carried a purse full of little Dum-Dum-type suckers, and she kept one in her mouth the whole ride. Aunt Linda had asked about her treatments and how she was feeling. Mom said she was managing everything well. Aunt Linda knew her sister well enough to know that her response wasn't true.

And then, all of Aunt Linda's worries were suddenly pushed to the background in the face of a much more immediate global concern.

That same morning, Al Qaeda terrorists crashed two planes into the World Trade Center, and the attack was all anyone talked about. Of course, the trip to Florida got canceled. Our family's concerns turned elsewhere. Allen got recalled to Virginia Beach that day and deployed on September 19 to support Operation Enduring Freedom in Afghanistan as a parachute rigger and third-class petty officer. The ship he was detached to, the USS

Theodore Roosevelt, did not enter a port for 159 days, a record for that vessel.

Communication with Allen was minimal and sporadic due to operational security. He couldn't call often, and someone had to grab the phone right then or it would be another couple of weeks before he could ring again. Mom hated to miss even one call from Allen. He wouldn't return until March 27, 2002. Our whole family turned out to see the ship pull into port, and the news interviewed a teary-eyed Dad and Mom about their son's return.

Of course, Mom's medical issues got swamped within the family in the wake of the terrorist attacks and Allen's part in the U.S. military action in the Middle East. Aunt Linda didn't pursue any more conversations about her sister's health. But she knew something was very, very wrong.

And she was about to discover a lot more information than she'd previously uncovered, information Uncle Mike had figured out five years earlier.

In 1996, before Aunt Linda married Mike, she had introduced him to our family at a little get-together at her home. Mike loved meeting everyone, but he was especially struck by Dad, and not in a good way. Mike thought Dad behaved oddly through the night, but he could see my mom was completely enamored with Dad.

It wasn't hard to see why she adored him. Tall, bearded, and full of masculine charm, Dad surrounded himself with friends everywhere he went. From his stint in the Navy as an aviation electronics technician to his career as a biomedical technician for the Veterans Administration, my dad won the hearts of nearly everyone who knew him.

If he occasionally made the odd comment, failed to show up for work, or spent more money than he actually had on hand, well … that was just Dad. He could turn the toughest situation into a joke. Mike, a serious and driven professional, didn't always appreciate Dad's strange humor or his quirky stories. But over time, he had grown to love my parents almost as much as Aunt Linda did.

After Uncle Mike married into the family, he noticed a gradual change in my mom. She grew to be inconsistent, like my dad, and a little on edge. Uncle Mike wondered aloud to Aunt Linda if my parents were having marriage problems, but Aunt Linda assured him that whatever was wrong, that was certainly not the issue. One thing they did agree on, however, was that they would help in any manner Mom would allow.

Mom, Dad, and brother shortly after Allen joined the Navy in 2000
(Just as my parent's medical problems started to accelerate)

A proud sister after my brother returned home
from one of his three deployments

11

Mostly Merry and Bright

Sunday, December 1, 2002
Rutgers

THE SUNDAY AFTER THANKSGIVING, I HEADED BACK TO RUTGERS as planned. According to Dad's doctors, he would be coming home in less than a week. The medical team at St. Albans had apparently straightened out whatever had gone wrong with his medicines.

I had no reason to stay in Virginia. Nothing I could do. Besides, as Mom said when she was ushering me out the door, I'd be back home for the winter break in less than a month.

At Rutgers, final exams came and went. I knew my parents would be proud of my grades, and I was happy about that.

I returned to Virginia as planned for Christmas. Mom surprised me with lots of clothes and some small things I wanted, nothing too lavish. At 18, I found more pleasure in spending time with my family than I did in anything they bought and wrapped for me. It was an especially meaningful holiday after my dad's brush with death just a month earlier.

Whatever medical problems Dad had experienced the previous month seemed to have evaporated. He joked around like he always did, still wearing his Dockers, button-up shirts, and navy blue sweaters. We got him a new one of those sweaters every year for Christmas.

I breathed a sigh of relief that everything was okay at home and once again boarded the train back to Rutgers the week after Christmas for my second semester. The gymnastics team had to be back on campus early to train for the start of the competition season.

According to the calendar that I later received in a stack of papers from the police, my parents left Virginia on Friday, January 24, 2003, headed for Rutgers University. Rutgers was hosting a quad meet against JMU, Towson, and Ursinus the next day. I had the opportunity to compete in exhibition routines on my best two events, floor and bars.

Even though I would compete, my performance wouldn't count toward the team score. Only the top six gymnasts were selected for the lineup for each event, and I just wasn't there yet. My routines were good, but they still needed work. That was okay with me. I was simply excited for my parents to watch me perform in my first collegiate competition.

As the event started and I looked up from my spot on the floor, I could see my dad snacking on the leftover pizza he'd saved from lunch. Both my parents looked really happy, and I was, too. The day couldn't have gone better. I turned in two great performances, nailing both routines. My parents were so, so proud of their little girl.

Coach Chollet-Norton took us out to eat at Old Man Rafferty's in downtown New Brunswick that night. She wanted to spend time with my parents and get to know them a little more. I wanted to spend time with them, too.

Mom and Dad booked a room at one of those old-school Howard Johnson's hotels, the bright orange kind, just right up the road from the Rutgers campus. I stayed with them while they were in town. Sunday was the last day I saw them, and we went out for lunch just to squeeze in a few more minutes together. I'm glad we did. So very, very glad we did.

In hindsight, I guess both Mom and Dad did seem a little tired that night, but I didn't think much of it. If anything else seemed out of the ordinary—if there was even one omen of what was happening at my house back in Newport—I didn't pick up on it. I had no idea of what was about to come my way.

12

The End of Rutgers?

Monday, March 17, 2003
Rutgers

THE REST OF JANUARY AND FEBRUARY PASSED UNEVENTFULLY. Then March came in like a lion.

I was on College Avenue with a few of my teammates. We had just finished up practice for the day and were going to grab lunch at Au Bon Pain. The dorms were closed because all the students were home on spring break, but our team was still on campus because we were in season.

I stepped away from my teammates to call my mom on my new cell phone. Nothing big. I just wanted to tell her about a new skill combination on bars that I was working on. She answered the phone a little coldly, but I plunged ahead.

When I started to tell her about the combination, she stopped me with a fierce declaration. "You're not going back to Rutgers next year."

"What?" I asked. Total shock.

"We can't afford it."

I knew they were in financial straits, but it never occurred to me that *their problems* would affect *my life.*

As she talked on and on, I groped for something that made sense—a lifeboat of sanity somewhere in her sea of words. I found nothing.

"We're going to sell the house…"

"Why?" I asked in even deeper shock.

"So it won't go into foreclosure."

"Where will you go?"

"A small house?" she said. "An apartment? I don't know, Lauren. We'll downsize somehow."

This tense and heated conversation was much different than our typical talks. With the way she spoke and the tone of voice she used, Mom made it sound like their financial problems were somehow my fault. She reminded me that they had paid all the fees associated with my gymnastics—not a cheap sport, especially at a national level—along with taking out loans for my tuition at Rutgers.

I felt hurt, humiliated, and confused. I'd worked and practiced for years, enduring pain and missing out on a normal childhood to be a top-ranked athlete. I had earned that gymnastics scholarship fair and square. They were the ones who had agreed to take out the Parent PLUS loan to cover the out-of-state tuition at Rutgers. I didn't ask them to do that; I had just figured it must be right if they did it.

Now they were going to lose their dream house in the country? All because of me? What had I done wrong? I thought they wanted me here, wanted me to be a college gymnast.

Mom and Dad had even cautioned me not to take a job to help out with the finances. "You focus on gymnastics and school," they always told me. "We'll take care of everything else."

I had done what they asked. Why was she taking this out on me?

She finished the call by reminding me, "You'll have to leave Rutgers, Lauren."

I gulped and said what I always said. "I love you, Mom."

"I love you, too," she snapped and hung up.

At the time, I was too hurt by my mom's tone and her words to take in much else. Knowing what I know now, though, I realize that Mom was still protecting me, just like she always had. The truth was much more dire than she had let on.

What I didn't know was this…

Just three weeks earlier, Mom had turned up at Uncle Mike and Aunt Linda's house, asking for a place to stay. From the moment she arrived, it was clear that things weren't going well at the Sisler home.

The Rorrers weren't sure what was wrong. They just knew something big was in the wind.

Uncle Mike thought Mom might leave Dad. If she did, he was willing to offer her a place to stay and a chance to get back on her feet. Aunt Linda, however, didn't think there was anything amiss between my parents. She told Uncle Mike that Mom was far too codependent to just up and leave Dad. Rather than a marital spat, Aunt Linda suspected that their financial crisis lay behind her sister's desire to get out of the house for a week.

Whether the problems were relational or financial, though, Mom was tight-lipped about them. Not even my aunt, her trusted older sister, could dig much information out of her. That didn't stop her from trying. Still, each time Aunt Linda pressed the matter, Mom provided the same non-answer: "I'm lonely."

It was hard living so far out in the country now that the children were grown, she told Aunt Linda. Why didn't she have any friends close by to do things with? It would help take her mind off her troubles.

My aunt agreed that Mom needed more social interaction and that being stuck so far out of town couldn't be good for her. Throughout that week, Aunt Linda planned fun trips to the mall and nearby eateries just for the two of them. She hoped my mom could figure out a way to get through this … whatever it was she was going through.

Uncle Mike, typically, was more direct in his efforts to help his sister-in-law. He told her straight out, "If you need a place to stay for a while, you've got one here with us."

At the time, Mom seemed grateful for Uncle Mike's offer, but a few days later, she asked Aunt Linda to drive her to the VA Medical Center where Dad worked. She would ride home with him, she said.

Aunt Linda hadn't much liked the idea of her sister going back without making any new plans or changing anything in her life. But as Uncle Mike often said, "You can't solve a problem if people don't want your help." So Aunt Linda wished Mom well and waved goodbye.

The next Wednesday, Mom called Aunt Linda again. She needed to get a lockbox, she said, because my dad was taking some of her prescriptions. If he didn't stop, then she wouldn't have enough medication to get her through the next 90 days when she could get a refill.

"Bring it over," Linda told her. "I'll keep it for you."

On Thursday, Dad dropped Mom off at Aunt Linda's on his way to work so the sisters could spend the day together before Linda left town to help out a family member. As they'd agreed, Mom brought her newly filled prescription of fentanyl over to Linda's.

"How long will you be gone?" Mom asked. The answer would determine how many fentanyl patches Mom needed to keep for herself. Mom counted out the correct number and slipped them into a lockbox to take home. Aunt Linda put the rest in a shipping box, taped it up securely, and wrote Mom's name on it. Aunt Linda stored this box on the shelf in her closet where my mom could find it if she needed to access it before her sister returned home.

Linda and Mom spent the rest of the day together, going out to lunch, and enjoying each other's company. Before they parted, Mom said she was really going to miss Linda while she was gone and couldn't wait for her to get back.

It was the last time Aunt Linda ever saw her sister alive.

Throbbing with worry, I called my dad later to tell him about my conversation with Mom. He stayed calm and assured me that everything was fine.

"Mom's medications ran out," Dad told me. "She was in a lot of pain. They got it resolved." He urged me not to distress myself about their financial issues.

I shouldn't have worried anyway. Mom couldn't stay mad—at least, not at me, and not for long. She called again a day later, and we laughed and chatted like normal. A card from her arrived in my mailbox on March 22nd.

Mom had a flair for greeting cards. When you received a card from her, you got her heart in the mail.

This card's cover featured a charming cat dressed in scuba gear. Inside, I read her beautiful script:

03/19/03

Dear Lauren,

Thought about you when I saw this card. You never did have much luck with cats!

I just wanted to say I am so sorry for the hurtful things I said to you on the phone. I was drowning in my own self-pity!

I am so very proud of you and your gymnastics! You have worked so very hard to get where you are! And you are going up!

You are smart, beautiful, and a true gift of God to everyone you come in contact with! You are so much more than I could ever hope to be!

Keep focused and go for the pot of gold at the end of the rainbow! You will make it.

I Love You!
Your Mom

It was the last card I ever received from her.

Dad's 52nd birthday rolled around on March 20. I was bummed I wouldn't be with him on his actual birthday, but I did what I could to celebrate him. I mailed him a card, an action which—along with my figure, face, and smile—served as undeniable proof that I was, and always will be, Lesley Sisler's daughter.

It was one of those funny cards for dads—The Top 10 Things I've Learned From My Dad. Inside, I wrote:

Daddy,

I thought this card was perfect. Especially #6 ... money doesn't grow on trees!

Well, I was just thinking about you and wanted to wish you a Happy Birthday! I wish I could be there to celebrate ... I guess this is the first year I haven't been able to wish you a happy birthday in person.

I will have to take you out when I come home in May! It can be on me since I will be making a little bit of money from working. Well, I hope things will work out with the financial stuff. I know it will. Just keep your head up and keep praying.

I love you and miss you and Mom a lot. I can't wait to spend time with you two over the summer. It will be nice.

Happy Birthday, Daddy! You are the BEST! I am the luckiest person to have you as a father. You have done so much for me and Allen, and I feel like we have turned out pretty good. And things will just keep getting better for you … I promise!

Love,
Little Lady Lauren

PS: I will buy you that truck when I'm a doctor.

Knowing their financial troubles continued to prey on his mind, I wrote my heart on that card. At 18, I had never held a job, written a check, or made a budget. But I wanted Dad to know that whatever the issues were, we would get through them as a family. I wanted to assure him that there was nothing God couldn't handle.

Dad knew God would help us, right?

He and Mom faithfully attended Oak View Christian Church, the congregation that met near our house in the country. The miniature brick church had pretty white doors, an oversized steeple, and a panoramic view of Virginia's forested mountains in the background.

Just a handful of people gathered there every Sunday. When I went, I always knew exactly how many had shown up the week before because someone counted and then slid the numbers into an old marquee at the front of the sanctuary. They did the same with the offering. Rarely did the church's income exceed $30 or its attendance rise above 25 souls in a single week.

But the people at that church loved God and each other, and they thrived on singing the old hymns together. Maybe Dad didn't have the best voice in the congregation, but he probably had the loudest one. He loved to sing, and he could belt out the tune to "Amazing Grace" above everyone else combined. I loved looking up at him while he boomed out the words of sin, forgiveness, and redemption through the mercy of God.

Yes, I told him in my letter, we would be fine. God would take care of whatever problems our family faced. *With God all things were possible*. The Bible—and the plaque in my dorm room—said it, so it had to be true.

It was a message I would need to rely on myself before the month was over.

My card arrived on Dad's birthday, and three days later, I called him and Mom in the evening when I knew they would both be home. I still felt a tiny bit nervous about this exchange after that one weird and awful call from my mom. To my relief, however, our conversation turned into one of the best heart-to-heart talks we'd ever had.

I told Mom about the new bar skill combination I was working on, which was what I had wanted to tell her the day she informed me they were losing the house. I explained that I'd changed the way I was practicing it.

Thankfully, I could tell her that I was experiencing some success and consistency. It hurt my parents to see me go through the injuries and the hardships that came with my gymnastics career. I felt grateful for any time I could share good news with them. When I told her I was starting to perform at a higher level, she seemed really excited to hear about my progress.

Mom handed the phone off to my father. He thanked me for the birthday card and told me how proud he was of me.

They knew I'd had some struggles because I had been injured— again—early in my gymnastics career at Rutgers. He talked about how he admired my motivation to continue pursuing my gymnastics career.

Before we hung up, Mom said, "I love you, Woe."

She handed the phone to Dad. He said it, too. "I love you, Woe." I told them I loved them back.

After I disconnected the call, I finished studying for my upcoming mid-term exams. Then I chatted with Kara for a while before setting my alarm, turning out the light, and falling into the last innocent sleep I would enjoy for the rest of my life.

13

Lauren, Your Mom Died

Sunday, March 23, 2003, 8:00 a.m.
Giles County, Virginia

MOM AND DAD'S NEIGHBOR, JOYCE KESSINGER, CALLED BE-fore church that Sunday morning. Joyce and her husband lived down Spruce Run, about a mile from our home.

Would the Sislers be coming to services this morning? Joyce wanted to know.

No, Dad told her, both he and Mom were down with mild cases of the flu. They didn't feel up to attending service that morning and didn't want to spread their illness to the rest of the congregation.

Joyce told Dad the church would pray for him and Mom before she disconnected the call. To Joyce, blissfully unaware of the situation unfolding less than a mile from her home, the day seemed to pass uneventfully.

My call had come through around 7 o'clock that night. At 10 o'clock, Allen called our parents. Again, Dad answered the phone. He told my brother that both he and Mom were down with the flu. They'd even missed church. In the bathroom, Mom paused from lighting candles. A long bath was one of her favorite relaxation strategies. She hoped the hot water might make her feel better. Mom took the phone and chatted briefly. Then, Allen said goodbye to our parents and hung up.

Neither Joyce nor Allen nor I had any premonition of the chain of events about to transpire in our family's home.

Sunday, March 23, 2003, 11:45 p.m.
Giles County, Virginia

Dad woke up just before midnight. He had dozed off while watching TV on the couch in the living room. He called for Mom. "Lesley?"

No answer came back.

Dad got off the couch and walked into their bedroom. "Lesley?"

Still no answer.

He headed for the kitchen and called a third time. "Lesley?"

The dimly lit house remained silent. Dad opened the side door and stepped onto the wraparound porch. There sat Mom slumped over in a chair, skin exposed to the crisp mountain air.

"Lesley?" He shook her with both hands. Her bare arms felt cold against his fingertips. She didn't respond.

Dad panicked. He grabbed both of her wrists and pulled her forward out of the chair. Mom's knees hit the porch's wooden floor hard enough to bruise them both. Still, she showed no signs of consciousness.

Dad tried to lift Mom in his arms, but she was heavier than she looked. Finally, he gave up on carrying her and just pulled her through the house and into their master bathroom. She was still cold. So, so cold. He checked for a sign of life. Nothing. He briefly considered the possibility that she was actually, really dead but immediately dismissed the thought. He couldn't live without her, so she couldn't be dead. Life as they knew it was going to shatter in the next few days, and he couldn't go on without her help.

Finally, he saw it. A breath! Or it looked like she took a breath anyway. *Good*, he thought. *You just keep breathing.*

Now certain—or at least, very hopeful—that Mom was still alive, Dad plugged the drain in the bathtub and cranked the cold water tap to full blast. While the icy water filled the tub, Dad pulled off Mom's slippers. A frigid bath was all she needed to bring her back. It was a remedy he'd found on the internet. He was nearly positive it would work.

Moving awkwardly in the bathroom's confined space, Dad peeled off Mom's slacks. During all his frantic activity, Mom never once moved on her own. When Dad lifted her arms, she felt unusually heavy for a trim, attractive woman. So heavy. And so cold.

He glanced at her abdomen and ribs. Even in his frantic state, wishing more than anything that Mom would open her eyes, Dad had to admit that he couldn't spot any respiratory movements. Clearly, Mom wasn't breathing although he was sure she had been just minutes ago.

Dad dashed into the kitchen and, just like I had done the past Thanksgiving, dialed the number everyone has been taught to call in an emergency. He told the 911 operator his address and said that his wife was "slightly unresponsive." With this not-quite-accurate information, the call receiver dispatched the rescue squad instead of a fully stocked ambulance.

Mom wouldn't be happy about this call when she came around, Dad knew, but he no longer had a choice. Their secret was coming out whether they wanted it or not.

Monday, March 24, 2003, 12:05 a.m.
Giles County, Virginia

EMT April Blankenship was still awake when the call came through asking for support for an unresponsive middle-aged female near Newport. Although she rarely ran that route, April wasn't busy and volunteered to go. Only 21 years old, April was a go-getter who loved the adrenaline rush of the sirens, the lights, and the quick thinking that make up an EMT's professional life.

The driver warned her that he'd been to this address a few months earlier when Butch Sisler, the man who lived there, had nearly died of a drug overdose. April wasn't afraid. "I'm going up there. What is he going to do? Throw a pill at me?"

Still, the driver, not a certified EMT himself, wouldn't proceed without getting a deputy to go with them. It took April and the driver just under 15 minutes to make the five-mile drive from the fire station to our house on Boars Head Trail, weaving and winding through hills and pastures the whole way.

They arrived to find my dad in a full-blown panic and Mom lying partially dressed beside the bathtub half full of cold water. First, Dad told April that his wife wasn't breathing when he found her. Then, he said she was. Then, he changed his mind again and said her breathing had been shallow.

For the first time, April wondered if coming on this call had been smart. Had this man who quietly struggled with substance abuse actually done something to his wife?

April had no other explanation for why a healthy woman in her 40s would abruptly stop breathing. She checked for both a respiratory rate and a pulse but found neither. Mom's skin felt cool and dry to the touch. She appeared blue, probably because her temperature had dropped to just under 92°F.

April could see that my mom wasn't "slightly unresponsive" as my dad had reported. She was dead and probably had been for more than an hour.

According to Dad's most recent claim, however, Mom had stopped breathing just a minute ago. He hovered frantically in the background while April noted Mom's vital signs, none of which showed any vitality. Nevertheless, Dad wouldn't be persuaded that his wife couldn't pull out of this state. April steeled herself for the impossible task of bringing this woman back to life.

She began CPR, hoping against all evidence that she would get a heartbeat. The only EMT present, April had no one to help in transporting her patient to a backboard or cot, so she knelt above Mom on the bathroom floor, performing the compressions that she was increasingly certain would do no good.

The driver called Blacksburg for support, and their paramedic team arrived quickly. Now working together, April and the local paramedics valiantly attempted to bring my vibrant 45-year-old mother back to life. They even cracked her ribs in an aggressive effort at CPR with bag-mask ventilation. When it was obvious that CPR was not going to work, they switched tactics.

They put Mom's cold body on an EKG machine, intubated her with an endotracheal tube, put in IVs with normal saline, and shot her full of epinephrine and atropine to try to restart her heart. At 1:17 a.m., one of the techs gave the first of four epi injections and three atropine injections. He gave the last injection at 1:47.

The team attached defibrillator pads and used an AED to analyze Mom for lethal heart rhythm. She was consistently asystole—lacking any heart rhythm at all. They tried using the defibrillator pads to deliver low-level electrical current to artificially force her heart to beat at 80 bpm. Despite all their efforts, the EKG reading never changed.

By now, April and the Blacksburg team had gone from delivering a real emergency response to putting on a show for the desperate husband who incessantly watched over their shoulders for signs of life from his wife.

Despite all their efforts, Dad remained in a state of panic, unable to accept that he was losing my mom. The technicians kept up their attempts long past any real hope of resuscitation, pulling out every tool in their kit.

It was during their efforts at intubation that one of the technicians discovered something of interest lodged in the back of Mom's throat. He bagged it as evidence.

Given that no breathing or heart rhythm had returned during their 94 minutes of work to revive the unresponsive woman, the technicians ceased their efforts and called the attending physician at Giles Memorial emergency room. They reported that she had been down for over an hour. The physician called the code.

My mother was declared dead at 1:58 a.m. on March 24, 2003.

The paramedic team loaded her body into the ambulance and headed for the hospital, carrying the evidence bag with them.

After a somber drive that felt longer than it should have, they arrived at the Montgomery hospital and prepared to unload the body. It was then that they realized that the driver had transported the team to the incorrect hospital—the doctor at Giles Memorial had been the one who called her death, so that is where they needed to deliver her body.

It took the attending physician and nurses some time to sort through the tangled story and figure out whom they had mistakenly delivered, but they eventually sent Mom's body and the EMTs back on the road in the opposite direction.

This is the craziest call I've ever been on, April thought as they pulled into the correct hospital, grateful for a chance to go home soon and finally catch a couple of hours of sleep.

As things turned out, April's night was about to get a lot crazier than she ever dreamed.

Monday, March 24, 2003, 3:30 a.m.
Rutgers

The cordless phone on the desk next to my bed rang me awake.

My alarm clock read 3:30 a.m. Still groggy from sleep, I peered at the caller ID. My parents. Why were they calling at this time of the morning?

I punched the *talk* button on the phone. "Hello?"

"Lauren?" It was my dad. "I need to talk to your brother."

So why was he calling me? I took a deep breath. "What's wrong?"

"I just need to talk to your brother." Dad didn't sound like himself. He seemed confused and uncertain. "I can't find his number anywhere."

This wasn't right. Something wasn't right, and Dad didn't want to tell me about it.

Allen was stationed in Norfolk, and he had been on watch. I figured he had probably fallen asleep an hour earlier, but I found my brother's number and read it out to my dad.

"I'll call you back in a few minutes." Dad disconnected before I could ask any more questions.

Sitting on my bed with the phone in my hands, I tried to guess what might be happening at my house that had Dad so distraught. Less than a minute later, the phone rang. The caller ID told me my parents' phone was calling again.

"I couldn't get in touch with your brother." The first words out of Dad's mouth scared me more than ever.

"Dad! What's wrong?"

He paused before answering me. When he finally replied, I wished he hadn't.

"Lauren, your mom died."

I understood his words, but I could not process the information. He and Mom and I had all just talked right before I went to bed. I'd told her I loved her. She'd said she loved me. Mom was just 45 years old. Other than spinal problems that flared up every now and then, she was healthy. She was compassionate. Loving. Beautiful. Mom couldn't be dead. Not my mom.

"I need you to call your brother." Dad was speaking again. "Tell him your mom died. He needs to make arrangements to get home as quickly as he can."

Dad was still talking, but my brain wasn't working. Or maybe it was working much too quickly. I couldn't think. All I could do was feel, and everything felt merciless.

"What happened?"

"I can't explain it now," Dad said. "Just get to Roanoke. I'll be at the airport to pick you up." With that, he hung up.

"Lauren, wake up." It was Kara. I don't remember when I started crying, but at some point after the phone call with Dad, the tears started flowing. I wasn't aware that it was happening or that my sobbing was loud enough to wake up my roommate.

I curled tighter into the fetal position. Kara shook me. "You're having a nightmare."

"It's not a bad dream!" I insisted. My mind was spinning out of control. "It's real. My dad just called. My mom died."

Kara didn't know what to say, but she somehow maneuvered me off the floor and seated me back on my bed. What do you do when your mom dies, you're in college, and it's 3:30 in the morning? Neither of us knew.

All I knew was that I felt confused. I was trying to convince myself that my father was absolutely telling the horrible truth while at the same moment telling myself that there was no way this could have happened. My thoughts were crashing into one another, and anger began to tumble into the mix and create one jumble of pain.

Focus. I needed to focus. That's what athletes do. We focus. I had to focus on the next step. What was it?

Call my brother. That's it. Dad told me to call Allen. I could do that. Kara sat beside me and put her arms around me as I punched in the numbers I had read aloud to my dad just minutes earlier.

This time, thank goodness, Allen answered. "Hello?"

"Mom died." I blurted it out without thinking of how abrupt the words sounded.

"What?!"

"Call Dad, Allen. Call him now. Mom died."

The minute I delivered the news to my big brother, I felt like everything evaporated out of my hands. I had done what I needed to do. Allen would call my dad. They would talk. They would take care of everything.

All I had to do was get home to my father where I could feel his embrace and he could assure me everything was going to be okay.

14

Everything Was Not Okay

Monday, March 24, 2003, 4:00 a.m.
Rutgers

GETTING HOME WAS GOING TO BE A BIG ENOUGH PROBLEM FOR me to solve without worrying about how Mom could be dead. Despite being painstakingly frugal with the funds my parents occasionally sent me, I had next to no money in my account and no credit card to buy a plane ticket. Kara, however, did have a card, and she handed it over without reservation.

Still trembling in shock, I looked up the number for Continental Airlines and called from our dorm room. "I've got to book a flight to Roanoke," I told the agent in a shaky voice after I finally got off hold. "I need to book this flight *right now*."

"Will you be flying out of Philadelphia or Newark?" the agent asked me.

"Which is closer?" I tried to compose my thoughts and failed spectacularly. "Which will get me home quicker?"

"Newark."

"Then, that's where I'm flying out of."

The ticket cost more than the $200 spending limit Kara's mom had set on her credit card. So I had to hang up with the agent. By this time, I'd spent more than half an hour on the phone trying to buy a ticket and still had nothing to show for it.

Thankfully, Aunt Linda called at that very moment, and I asked her for advice. "Kara's mom can raise the limit on her card so you can get home," Aunt Linda told me. "Call and ask her to do that right now. Tell her I'll reimburse her for the cost of the ticket."

Aunt Linda hung up so Kara could use the phone to call her mom — yet another person to be awakened in this horrible string of calls. While I waited for Kara's mother to get a temporary exception from her credit card company, I surveyed my open closet.

"Kara?" I looked over my outfits. "What will I wear to my mom's funeral?"

Kara didn't know. Neither of us could think that far ahead. So I grabbed a bag and began stuffing it with every top, dress, and pair of pants I could while still being able to zip the suitcase. I mean … what do you need to take home from college when your mom dies in the middle of the night?

Finally, with help from Kara's mother, I snagged a ticket on the next flight for Roanoke leaving out of Newark. I called Aunt Linda back with the flight details, confident she would convey the news to my dad. All that was left was to get to the airport, which seems simple, but I didn't have a car on campus, and neither did Kara. Our friend Kraig Feldman did, though. I called his room from our phone.

"What's wrong?" Kraig asked when he finally picked up.

"My mom died," I said for the fourth time in less than an hour. "I need a ride to the airport."

Kraig asked no questions. "I'll take you."

Kara and I grabbed my suitcase, darted out of our door, ran through Clothier Hall, and clunked our way down the stairs, dragging the luggage behind us. We paid no attention to the commotion we made at that hour of the morning. When your mom dies in the middle of the night, you are allowed to not concern yourself with the rules of courtesy.

One floor down from ours, I pounded on Kraig's door. He opened it, clad in nothing but boxer shorts and still rubbing sleep from his eyes. "Let me get dressed. I'll get my car. It'll take a few minutes since it's in another lot across campus."

Kara and I waited for him in the dorm's lobby.

While I stood there surrounded by suitcases, I thought about what lay ahead of me. I hoped that if I got to Roanoke quickly enough, Mom wouldn't be dead. I could help Dad see that he had been wrong. And if she was — if she really was dead — at least I would be with my dad. He would hold me and comfort me. My dad would ease the pain and get me through this. I was Daddy's little girl.

Monday, March 24, 2003, 4:00 a.m.
Roanoke, Virginia

Uncle Mike was working the night shift in the emergency department at Carilion Roanoke Memorial Hospital, an hour away from Boars Head Trail, when Dad called with the news of Mom's death. Pulling on his 15 years of experience as an ER doctor, Uncle Mike tried to calm Dad down and get information out of him.

Yes, Dad told Mike, he had called me up at Rutgers. I knew what had happened. He had asked me to call Allen since he couldn't get through. No, Dad hadn't spoken to Allen personally yet.

Right then, another call came through for Dad, so the conversation ended abruptly, leaving Uncle Mike to ponder the devastating news.

With such a sudden and shocking death, Mike knew there was much more to the story than the few details Dad had shared. Mike had his suspicions, and he hoped that after such a tragedy my dad would come clean. In Mike's experience, Dad had never been very forthcoming, not even about the most mundane events. He was a warm, personable man but not always a precise one.

Uncle Mike called his friend and colleague Dr. Scott Hayes, local medical examiner for Giles County, to confirm the news. Scott hadn't heard anything about it, and surely my mom would have been brought to the morgue by now if what Dad said was true. He would check on the situation and let Mike know.

Standing in the emergency department, Uncle Mike waited impatiently for either Scott or Dad to call him back.

Monday, March 24, 2003, 4:15 a.m.
Giles County, Virginia

Vicky Jones, the nursing supervisor at Giles Memorial Hospital, called Dr. Scott Hayes minutes after he had hung up with Uncle Mike. She delivered the news that her staff had just transported a woman's body to the morgue.

According to Vicky, the body was that of Mrs. Lesley Sisler. She had probably been dead for close to five hours. Her husband, Butch, had just pulled into the hospital. He was willing to talk to Dr. Hayes as soon as the doctor arrived at the hospital.

Yes, Vicky would get Mr. Sisler's number and have it ready for the doctor when he arrived later in the morning. In the meantime, she would advise the decedent's husband that he would receive a call from the medical examiner.

An ER nurse then called LifeNet, an organ donation center that also provided emergency communication support for members of the military. The nurse gave LifeNet news that she had a previously healthy 45-year-old woman in the morgue. They needed to move fast if they wanted to get the family's permission to donate her organs to transplant patients. The ER nurse told them to use the home phone number to call the husband, Mr. Sisler. The son was in the military, she said. Perhaps LifeNet could help connect him with the family, too.

At 4:30 that morning, my father left the hospital. The charge nurse watched him go and recorded the time. She didn't notice when he returned 30 minutes later nor when he finally departed for the last time.

Monday, March 24, 2003, 4:35 a.m.
Giles County, Virginia

Half an hour after Uncle Mike had hung up with Dad, Scott Hayes called Mike and confirmed his worst fears.

Lesley Sisler had been brought by ambulance to Giles Memorial Hospital at 4:30 a.m. She was dead on arrival. In fact, she had been dead for hours, but a miscommunication with the ambulance driver had sent her first to the wrong hospital.

Her body had been assigned to the medical examiner's office. They would perform the autopsy the next morning in Roanoke.

Uncle Mike thanked his colleague and dialed Dad's number. No answer. He hung up and called his wife who was out of town helping a family member take care of her grandchildren while her daughter had surgery. He told her the news.

"Have you called my parents?" Aunt Linda asked him, still reeling from the blow of what had happened to her sister.

No, but he would. As soon as he hung up with Aunt Linda, Mike dialed Gramps and Grandma with the news that their beloved youngest daughter had passed away unexpectedly in the night. Gramps' distraught tone when he answered the phone told Uncle Mike that they had already received a call from Dad.

Mike rang Dad's number again. No answer. He dialed another time. No answer. Over and over, Mike called his brother-in-law's home phone. No one ever answered.

15

Uncle Mike, Where's My Dad?

Monday, March 24, 2003, 5:45 a.m.
Newark, New Jersey

THE TRIP TO THE NEWARK AIRPORT TOOK 45 MINUTES, BUT IT felt like forever as we drove down the Garden State Parkway. Normally charismatic and friendly, Kraig said little as he chauffeured us. Kara sat scrunched in the back of Kraig's black Acura. She, too, was quiet. I slumped in my seat and watched the electrical wires swoop up and down outside the passenger window.

While I was familiar with physical pain, I was only barely acquainted with grief. Unaccustomed to and unprepared for death, I grappled for a solid thought to hang onto. No one should die yet.

If either of my parents was going to go earlier than expected, it was supposed to be my dad. He had struggled with cholesterol and high blood pressure for years. Heart disease ran in his family. Plus, he had nearly a seven-year head start on my mom in age. Yes, he should have been the one to die first, years down the road.

In the back of my mind, I always imagined Mom would be devastated without him, of course, but she would make it. She had to. She was the glue that held us together.

Dad was the spender. Mom was the saver. Dad liked big toys. Mom liked tight budgets. "Reel it in, Butch," she always told him when he got excited about a new truck. He had promised me that he'd help me buy my dream car, a Mercury Cougar with a big spoiler on the back. Mom told him not to make promises he couldn't deliver.

If Mom were gone, who would reel us in?

As I rode in Kraig's car, I counted down the hours until I could jump in my father's arms and hear him tell me it was all going to be okay. I could handle everything I was feeling about losing my mom if I could just feel my dad's embrace. I needed Dad to help me navigate this. I needed him to help me get back up off the mat.

Monday, March 24, 2003, 8:15 a.m.
Newark Liberty International Airport

At the airport, I checked my luggage through to Roanoke and found my seat on the plane. As soon as I sat down, I started sobbing for the first time since Kara pulled me off the floor of our room hours earlier. I knew people were looking. They were worried. I tried to stop shaking and crying in my seat. I couldn't.

The flight attendant, a pretty, blonde woman, asked me what was wrong.

"My mom just died," I told her. "I'm on my way home."

"Why don't you come up front with me?" she said. "You can sit in first class."

I appreciated her kindness, but the first-class assignment was wasted on me. I was just as miserable in the roomy, cushy seat as I would have been stored with the luggage. I stared out the window at the clouds below me. *Is this where my mom is now? Above the clouds? With me? Watching me?*

My brain attacked me with questions. *What if this isn't real? What if I land and my mom's at the airport? Maybe Kara is still trying to wake me up from a nightmare. Maybe this will end.*

Hours later, the plane touched down in Roanoke. I disembarked with the rest of the passengers and made my way to find my dad. As we walked off the plane, the airport music greeted us, and Elton John's song "Rocket Man" came over the speakers. The lyrics about being lonely in space on a timeless flight struck me.

It really would be a long, long time 'til touchdown.

Mom loved Elton John.

Outside the Roanoke airport, I looked for our car in the line of traffic. I was about to float out into space, and I needed my dad to reel me back in, back down to earth.

A black Jeep Cherokee pulled up to the curb.

Uncle Mike and Justin stepped out of it. They wrapped me in a hug, and as they held me close, I felt a small piece of my tension drift away. I was finally home, finally with my family, and finally able to cry with people who understood. All I needed now was to see my dad.

Justin carried my suitcase to the back of the car, and Uncle Mike grabbed my carry-on bag. I got in the backseat.

We had driven about 100 yards from the crowded entrance of the airport before I realized something wasn't right with this scene. They weren't supposed to be the ones to pick me up.

"Uncle Mike?" I leaned forward in my seat. "I just want to see my dad. Where is he?"

Mike looked at Justin and pulled the Cherokee over to the side of the road. I can still feel the soft bounce of the gravel under the tires. Mike put the vehicle in park, turned in his seat, and looked directly into my eyes.

"Lauren, your dad died, too."

I took the news calmly. I let the tragedy wash over me stoically, without a gush of tears or an outcry of shock. Maybe I had already used up all my tears on the flight; maybe my cup was full to the brim of sorrow, leaving me no room to expand my grief any further.

Somehow, I think I knew what had happened when Uncle Mike—instead of Dad—stepped out of that Cherokee at the airport. A few silent tears rolled down my cheeks as Mike turned on his blinker to get back on the road, but they quickly dried up. I realized without a doubt that this was real; this was not a nightmare. My tears could change nothing. Hours of crying didn't bring Mom back, and I felt no better for it.

Uncle Mike and Justin drove me to my grandparents' house. Aunt Linda was still on her way from visiting relatives in Tennessee. Uncle Mike quickly retreated behind a closed door—he had things to take care of at home, calls to make that he didn't want me to overhear.

16

This Has Got to Be a Nightmare

Monday, March 24, 2003, 5:45 a.m.
Giles County, Virginia

DAD ARRIVED AT OUR HOME FROM THE HOSPITAL BEFORE SUN-rise. He turned on several lights, flipped on the television, and walked into their master bathroom. The tub was still half-filled with tepid water where he'd tried to shock Mom back to life several hours earlier. Mom's scented candles that she had lit now sat cold around the bathroom. Then, Dad strolled into the kitchen.

He opened the freezer. Their stash of products still beckoned. Just one ice-cold moment and then hours of pain-free bliss awaited. He turned away from the temptation and picked up the cordless phone.

Dad tried to call Allen again so they could figure out their next steps, but the call didn't go through. He made several other attempts to call my brother, but everything was growing more difficult. Dad felt his fingers become clumsy with the phone's buttons. No point in holding out any longer. He went back to the freezer and helped himself.

The phone in his hand abruptly rang. It was a representative from LifeNet. She introduced herself as Robin and said she needed to know if Mr. Sisler was willing to donate his deceased wife's organs to transplant patients. Robin could also help him contact his son who was now stationed in Norfolk, VA, with the Navy. Dad felt grateful for the assistance.

Robin just needed Allen's social security number, she said. Dad excused himself from the phone and started toward the office where he and Mom kept their personal documents in a file. It was the last thing he ever did.

Monday, March 24, 2003, 5:50 a.m.
Giles County, Virginia

Giles County Sheriff's Deputy Dispatcher Judy Martin received a call from a woman named Robin. Robin explained that she worked for LifeNet and she had recently contacted Butch Sisler, the man who had discovered his wife's body slumped on his front porch hours earlier.

As part of the usual LifeNet procedure, Robin had asked Mr. Sisler for his son's social security number. He had excused himself briefly from the phone to go locate it. He never returned. Instead, Robin heard a fall and loud snoring, so she disconnected. Could the sheriff's office do a wellness check on Mr. Sisler?

Judy dispatched Deputies Ted Vaughn and Eric Thwaites to the Sisler home to discover why Mr. Sisler had not returned to the phone. They made the trip in 26 minutes. The deputies announced themselves as they opened my family's front door. No one answered.

Inside the home, Deputies Vaughn and Thwaites found Dad lying prone on the kitchen floor, the top of his head pointed at the refrigerator. His right arm rested by his head, and his left arm lay by his side. A cordless phone sat facedown on the floor next to him. Near his mouth, blood and sputum had pooled, probably from where he either coughed or vomited.

Deputy Vaughn turned my dad over. It was obvious to the deputies that Dad had hit his face on the corner of the kitchen countertop when he fell. They checked for a pulse. He was unresponsive and not breathing. Deputy Vaughn immediately began examining Dad while Deputy Thwaites called for an ambulance. One was already on its way, the dispatcher told him.

Monday, March 24, 2003, 6:15 a.m.
Giles County, Virginia

This has got to be a nightmare, April Blankenship thought as the exact same address scrolled across her screen again. *That woman just died. I took her to the hospital morgue myself—twice.*

Wondering what on earth was going on, April again answered the call. Sure enough, a male had been found unresponsive. "There is something wrong with the people who live in that house," April told her husband. "This does not happen."

This time, April drove herself to Boars Head Trail, her second visit in less than six hours. She entered the house within minutes of the deputies. Deputy Vaughn had already checked Dad for a pulse, so April hooked him to a monitor. Her patient was in asystole with no detectable heartbeat.

"How long has he been down?" she asked, noticing his pupils had fully dilated.

No one knew for sure. At least 30 minutes.

"Has he made any response to you?"

"None."

With no more information than that to go on, April called the hospital for directions.

"You might get his heart rate back," the doctor told her, "but his brain function is irretrievable."

"He's just 52," April said.

"But his chances of a meaningful recovery are almost nil," the physician explained. "If you do bring back his heartbeat, the family will have an awful choice to make. Do not do CPR."

April didn't.

My dad was declared dead at 7:08 on the same morning my mom died. The Blacksburg EMTs transported his body to the same morgue they had taken her to just five hours earlier.

For the first time, April relaxed enough to really look around a house she now half suspected might be haunted. *I'd love to live here* was the thought that unexpectedly popped into her head. The place was comfortable, beautifully furnished, and obviously filled with love. What could possibly have gone so tragically wrong?

Deputy Thwaites was having similar thoughts as he explored our house. In no time, though, he met a mountain of evidence—prescription narcotics, all in my parents' names but far more than two people could possibly need, no matter their medical condition. It was no mystery what had happened. As long as there was no crime to report, however, there was nothing more for him to do. The deputies took the pills with them to the station, but the family would be left to clean up the rest of the evidence.

Monday, March 24, 2003, 7:30 a.m.
Roanoke, Virginia

Unsuccessful in his attempts to reach his brother-in-law, Uncle Mike finally called Judy Martin, the sheriff's dispatcher in Giles County.

Judy reported the news he didn't want to hear. Butch Sisler was dead. "It looks like it might be a suicide, Mike," she told him. "The sheriff's on his way over there. I'll call you when we know more."

Uncle Mike hung up the phone and tried to process what had just happened. Butch *and* Lesley. Both dead. Gone on the same night. Flying 36,000 feet overhead, I had no idea I had just become an orphan.

The phone in Mike's hand rang. *Allen Sisler* popped up on the caller ID. Mike sighed and answered.

"I keep calling home over and over, but I haven't been able to reach Dad," Allen said. "Have you heard from him?"

"Allen, your father is dead."

Mike barely heard Allen's whisper. "What are we going to do now?"

As a long-time emergency room physician, Uncle Mike spent his days going from room to room, telling people that their loved ones had passed away. He was an expert at delivering bad news. He knew not to pull punches, not to give false hope, but he also knew how to deliver bad news in a way that loved ones could handle.

Sometimes, Mike directed nurses to inform patient families that the medical team was "doing everything we can, but it doesn't look good," even when he knew the patient was already dead. Things like that gave people time to process the inevitable.

But he knew I had no time at all. No nurse could run interference for him. And even though he had delivered devastating news countless times before, it did not prepare him for what he would have to tell his own niece later that day.

Mike drove home from the hospital and made a plan. Instead of Dad, he would pick me up at the airport, but he wouldn't do it alone. He would take his stepson, Justin, with him. Justin and I had been thick as thieves since we were kids. It might help me, Uncle Mike thought, to have my cousin there for support when he delivered the news.

Ever methodical, Mike planned his approach before he got to the airport. He wouldn't tell me about Dad until he could get me away from the crowd at the doors. Barely 18 years old, naïve, sheltered, and used to earning all the things I wanted, Uncle Mike worried I might completely lose it when I heard that my dad had died five hours after my mom.

I didn't lose control. I lost everything else.

17

Who Will Love Me Now?

Monday, March 24, 2003, 3:00 p.m.
Roanoke, Virginia

M Y GRANDPARENTS GRIEVED OPENLY. ONE OF THE FEW THINGS
I remember from that day is their complete distress. They almost
seemed like children, lost in their overwhelming grief that was
just as intense as my own, yet they expressed it unguardedly.

Their grief stung almost as much as my own. I had spent so many
summers at their house watching soap operas or *The Price is Right,* sometimes going to the pool at their townhome after gymnastics practices.

Aunt Linda's car eventually pulled into the townhouse parking space
late that afternoon. She ushered me into one of the guest bedrooms so I
could fall apart on her.

How did this happen? Where do I go from here? Do I stay at Rutgers?
Do I keep doing gymnastics? What happens to the house? So many unknowns to this new reality. So many holes to fill. So many moments and
milestones that lay ahead. So many dreams tarnished with the fear of the
unknown and the fear of all that was lost.

Lying on the bed next to Aunt Linda, I blurted out, "Nobody will ever
love me or want to marry me because I don't have parents."

It puzzles me even now when it pops up in my memories. Why in that
moment—with both my parents dead in a shocking way—*why* would I
think about getting married when I didn't even have a boyfriend?

Perhaps I was already searching for that unconditional love that my
parents showed me for 18 years. How could I replace that? Who would love
me now that they were gone?

By late afternoon, my grandparents' house had started filling up with friends and their parents. I specifically remember my closest childhood friends and club gymnastics teammates being the first to show up.

Before long, Aunt Linda had had her fill of a dozen weepy teenage girls along with distraught elderly parents all under one roof. She called me over to her and put a folded bill in my hands. "Take this money, and go to the Country Store for ice cream with your friends."

I gaped at Benjamin Franklin's picture on the $100 bill she handed me. "Aunt Linda, ice cream doesn't cost $100, not even for a dozen people."

"Put the change in your wallet, Woe." Her eyes filled with tenderness. "You're going to need money."

When we lived in Roanoke, Mom had often taken me to the Country Store for ice cream. I liked to pick out my own flavors and cram as many toppings on my serving as I could. I always ordered the chocolate-and-vanilla swirl yogurt with cookie dough and sprinkles, but Mom preferred the lighter flavors—sorbets, creamsicles, and plain vanilla.

I took the money Linda gave me and treated my friends to ice cream. The bill came to just over $25. I passed Mr. Franklin over to the cashier who gave me my change. I had never held so many bills in my hand at one time in my entire life. But I did as Aunt Linda said and tucked the $75 into my wallet.

At least, I had cash now, and that felt good. I couldn't imagine, though, what I would use that much money on.

Tuesday, March 25, 2003
Roanoke, Virginia

"$3,700!"

I was floored. I wiped the tears off my cheeks and the snot from my nose before I repeated the number. "$3,700?"

The funeral director blankly looked at me, then at Allen, and finally at Aunt Linda. She and Uncle Mike had agreed that the service would be exactly what Allen and I wanted, and what we wanted was to honor our parents in a way that fit their style.

Our parents would have an open casket and a full service, Allen and I decided. Nothing was too good for them. Allen and I—broke though we were—spared no expense to honor our parents. We brushed aside Aunt Linda's gentle suggestions that we might honor them just as well on a budget.

Dad loved flashy cars and sprawling houses. He took pride in his job and his service in the Navy. He was a big man with a big personality and bigger ambitions. Everything Butch Sisler did was larger than life.

My dad never took "no" for an answer in his life, and he wasn't getting second best from me. We rented a simple oak casket to use for the ceremony and selected a black onyx urn that would eventually hold his remains and be his final resting place. He loved the sleek look of that stone.

And Mom? Lesley Sisler didn't step outside her door until she was put together. I mean *put together*: styled hair, polished nails, and matching outfit. Her look was often casual, but it was always fashionable. Despite some recent health problems, Mom had kept her healthy figure and sense of style.

I picked out an urn fashioned from a cream-colored marble, thinking it would match her low-key but elegant taste. Like Dad, she would also lie in a simple oak casket for the ceremony.

Fortunately, Mom and Dad had already chosen—and paid for—burial plots in the nearby veterans' cemetery in Amelia Court House, Virginia. Mom had told Aunt Linda how much they'd admired the peaceful setting and even enjoyed their packed lunches with the caretaker in his offices after looking over the grounds.

That left me to make my first major adult purchase—two caskets, two urns, and a funeral program. For all that, I would be up to my ears in debt, and I didn't even know how to write a check. Not that it mattered. Any check I wrote then would have bounced sky-high.

My brother and I agreed to split the costs of the service. When the funeral director added up our selections, he handed us a total bill of $7,400. Half was Allen's part. Half was mine.

The $75 in change from the ice cream store the day before hadn't lasted long.

After the arrangements were taken care of, Mike and Linda took me back to their house where friends and family could keep me distracted. Then, they drove the 45 minutes between their home in Roanoke and my family's house in Giles County.

The minute Mike had called with the news of Lesley's death, Aunt Linda put together the biggest pieces of the puzzle. She knew what was probably in that house, and she wasn't about to let me or Allen be the one to discover the evidence.

Aunt Linda didn't know it, but she was too late. Allen and his friend Matt Dunne had beaten her to the house and had already scouted out the place. When they'd arrived, Allen had noticed the answering machine's light blinking. He pressed *play*.

All his frantic calls to his father from the night before tumbled out first. Then, he heard a message dated the previous Friday, a conversation between our parents that was recorded when Mom didn't get to the phone before the answering machine kicked on. Dad had called from work to ask what they would eat for dinner. They gave no clues about what was happening. The conversation seemed so normal it felt eerie.

Then, Allen spotted something on the kitchen floor. He picked it up.

"What is it?" Matt asked.

"A toe tag."

When Aunt Linda arrived, however, her quest was for something less gruesome but no less important. At her sister's home, Linda walked straight to the bedroom to pick out appropriate clothes for Mom and Dad to wear in the open caskets we had decided on. While she searched for the best clothes, she made sure to leave everything in the home exactly as Deputy Thwaites had written up in his report.

Aunt Linda found dozens of wrappers and lollipop sticks beside the bed, the remains of Mom's collection of pain-control suckers—the same ones she carried with her on 9/11 when they had planned to go to Florida. The same ones that were "not a problem."

Joyce Kessinger, the neighbor who had called and asked about church the same morning of Mom's death, had already scrubbed the kitchen floor to remove all traces of blood and bile from where Dad had fallen—not the typical neighborly favor, but Aunt Linda was grateful for her help.

After securing the clothing items, she and Uncle Mike scoured the entire house for other things. They located the stash of empty prescription drug bottles in the bathroom, the remains of a mountain of fentanyl suckers, and even a razor blade and pill crusher under the sink.

In the kitchen, Uncle Mike and Aunt Linda discovered another trove of information. Aunt Linda picked up a piece of paper on the counter. She read the fine print on the document and then showed the date to Uncle Mike. It was a prescription for narcotics. Dad had filled it just a few weeks earlier, the very day Mom had abruptly ended her stay with Uncle Mike and Aunt Linda and insisted on going home.

"Now we know why Lesley wanted to leave our house and come home with Butch," Aunt Linda said.

The lockbox Aunt Linda had loaned Mom just days earlier to keep her fentanyl patches safe now sat on the counter, its lid open and its interior empty. Those patches were powerful prescription narcotics designed to be worn on the chest for time-released delivery. Mom and Dad had polished off a two-week supply in a matter of days.

Uncle Mike and Aunt Linda carefully gathered up each piece of evidence that my parents were abusing drugs. With all the suggestions of wrongdoing out of the house, they could take their time telling me the truth.

With Allen at Mom and Dad's burial site in Amelia Court House, Virginia

18

One Set of Footprints

Thursday, March 27, 2003, 7:00 p.m.
Oakey's Funeral Home

KARA CAME FOR THE FUNERAL, AS DID MANY OF MY FRIENDS from Rutgers. Coach Chollet-Norton had to get special approval from the NCAA, but Rutgers was able to fund travel for some of my teammates to come to the service in Virginia.

So many out-of-town friends came and crashed at Aunt Linda's house that you couldn't walk through the living room without stepping on someone in a sleeping bag. To top it off, the air conditioner broke, and they all sizzled under an unseasonable hot spell. I didn't notice any of it.

Preparing for a funeral was the most awful thing I'd ever done, worse than learning the terrible truth about my parents' deaths. How was I, in a few days' time, supposed to properly plan a memorial for the people who had spent 18 years dedicating their lives and their love to me? How could the insignificant choices about flowers and funeral programs represent the totality of their lives?

I did the best I could.

Aunt Linda had given pictures of my mom to the mortuary cosmetologist. She had also bought me a dress since nothing Kara and I picked out in our trauma-induced panic at 3:30 a.m. really worked for a funeral.

As a family, Aunt Linda, Allen, and I slipped into the funeral home for an early viewing before the crowds arrived. My parents' two caskets sat side by side on the front right of the long, rectangular-shaped room. I almost lost my composure before I got to the front.

An open-casket funeral might not have been a great idea after all. Lying in their coffins, my parents looked like the saddest people I'd ever seen.

I couldn't stand the thought that Mom and Dad's last moments in this world had been so terribly, unutterably hopeless that they still looked so despondent even with all of the funeral home's efforts to beautify them for the embalming.

At 18 years old, I didn't realize that they looked the same as all deceased people. Their faces were expressionless—blank canvases waiting for someone to give them an emotion.

Dad and Mom weren't terribly, unutterably sad.

I was.

People packed out the funeral home and stood wall-to-wall at the service. A crowd even gathered outside.

Mom always told Aunt Linda she wanted more friends, but she should have seen the number of people who showed up to honor her that day.

On the day of the memorial—one year to the day after Allen returned from active-duty service in the Middle East—my aunt and I had planned to each speak, and together, the congregation would sing, pray, and read scriptures.

Just before Aunt Linda was slated to deliver the eulogy, my mom's brother, Ross Dornbush, would read the words of St. Paul:

> The bodies we now have are weak and can die. But they will be changed into bodies that are eternal. Then the Scriptures will come true, "Death has lost the battle! Where is its victory? Where is its sting?" Sin is what gives death its sting, and the Law is the power behind sin. But thank God for letting our Lord Jesus Christ give us the victory! (1 Cor. 15:54–57, CEV)

We would have two songs—Alabama's "Angels Among Us" for my dad and Eric Clapton's "Tears in Heaven"" for Mom.

Then, it would be my turn. I had handwritten my remarks in orange marker on lined notebook paper. I would read them verbatim from the front, and then I planned to recite my favorite poem, "Footprints," mostly from memory. I had relied on that poem for the courage I needed to face my biggest challenges, which had been gymnastics meets up until a few days ago. I wished that I could still have that naïvety.

How ironic that I would be reciting a poem about footprints, yet I decided I would walk alone. I would stand in front of the congregation of friends and family and speak at my parents' funeral by myself. After reciting the poem, I planned to give a short speech: "My parents have guided my brother and me down the right path, and now it's time for us to take what they have given us and make them proud by achieving all our goals in life."

To honor my father's time in the military, there would be the traditional playing of "Taps," while the military representatives ceremonially folded the flag on my father's casket and presented it to the next of kin. I had figured Allen would be the one to receive the flag, but he wanted to stand and give our father his final salute. According to military protocol, he could not receive the flag and salute at the same time, so Allen asked that the flag be handed to me. I was surprised, honored, and horribly sad, just as all military family members are when they receive that dreaded bundle of stars and stripes.

It felt like forever as I stood in that receiving line hugging everyone who came through and hearing their condolences. When I finally got to embrace Kara, she assured me that I did a wonderful job on the eulogy. She didn't think I could make it through that, but I did, and she was proud of me. I wasn't sure that I had done well. By then, it had all begun to blur around me. I only knew that I didn't have parents, and other people did have questions. Lots of them. Questions I couldn't answer. I didn't know. Or want to know.

The only thing I knew for sure was that I needed to stay here with my family. I would miss Kara's friendship, the team, and all the fun we had, but no way was I going back to Rutgers.

19

Contradictions and the Reality of Grief

I FLEW BACK TO RUTGERS ON APRIL 3RD. AFTER MY PARENTS' FU-
neral, I had insisted to my family that I stay in Virginia near the memories with my parents. Aunt Linda was equally insistent that I needed to
return to Rutgers. We'd held our final discussion on the subject while sitting in the car inside her garage.

"Lauren," Linda had told me, "it's time you went back to school."

I don't remember how I responded, but my aunt told me later that I
"flipped out."

She tried reasoning with me. "What will you do here in Roanoke?"

I didn't have an answer ready for her, so Aunt Linda pressed her advantage. "When you went to Rutgers, you made a commitment to your
coach. You made a commitment to your team. And you made a commitment to your school. You need to go back and honor those commitments."

When Aunt Linda talked about commitment, honor, and keeping your
word, she was speaking my language. I weakened in my resolve to stay in
Virginia.

Later, I learned that Aunt Linda had been in touch with Chrystal Chollet-Norton who had agreed to set up therapy and a full emotional support
system for me at Rutgers. It was much more than I would have in Giles
County if I remained behind to serve as the unpaid curator of my parents'
memories.

After our talk, I agreed to go back to college. At the same moment, I
both wanted to stay in Virginia and leave as quickly as possible, which is a
contradiction, but a reality of grief. If I wanted to admit the truth—which I
didn't—Rutgers just felt like a good place to run away to.

And if there was one thing I wanted to do in the days after my parents' funeral, it was to run. Away from reality, away from God. And maybe most importantly, away from my own questions: *How could this happen to me? How could this happen to my family? How could God allow this to happen to the two people who loved me the most?*

I had no answers, but I did have support from my friends and family around Virginia and up at Rutgers. They took up a collection for me, and I purchased clothes, toiletries, snacks, and other necessities of college life. Aunt Linda drove me to the bank to open an account and taught me how to write a check.

Back at Rutgers, Chrystal Chollet-Norton and Kate Hickey, the senior associate athletics director, helped me set up financial aid so I wouldn't run out of tuition, room, and board money. And my friends and teammates did their best to support me, but how can anyone, no matter how kind or well-intentioned, replace your mom and dad?

The gym became my refuge, but even there, grief would find me. During gymnastics practice, I would sit in the corner and sob with grief. Sometimes the coaches would make me get up and join the team for practice. On other days, they let me cry it out.

In the afternoons, I would return to my dorm, and in my room, I would slip into a make-believe world where my parents were still alive. Often, I hoped Kara wouldn't be there so I could just be alone for a bit and talk to my parents. I would pick up the phone on my desk and pretend to hold conversations with Mom and Dad. It was one way I could escape the cold and hollow reality of my life.

I had recorded their answering machine message on my computer so I could listen to my mom's voice over and over. I wanted so badly to hear her voice for real. I wanted the automated voice on the answering machine to suddenly buzz with life. I wanted to pick up the phone and listen to her say she loved me one more time. Even with all the pretend conversations I held with Mom and Dad, nothing could ease the pain or make up for their loss in real life.

Maybe Kara suspected what I was up to and kindly made it a point to give me some extra space. It would be like her to do that; she had always been supportive and gracious. Without her, I don't know how I would have gotten home in the first place.

Not everyone was as sensitive as Kara, however, but I couldn't exactly blame them. After all, few people know how to handle a girl whose parents both died on the same night.

One day, I overheard one of my teammates talking to her mom on the phone. Their voices got louder, and my teammate's words got uglier. Finally, she shouted some terrible things at her mom and slammed down the phone. My teammate looked me dead in the eye and said, "I hate my mom sometimes."

It was like a punch in the gut. I wanted to lash out, to tell her how wrong she was, how lucky she was to have a mom to call—the only phone calls I got to have with my mom were imaginary. I thought back to that tough conversation with my mom a week before she died. Even though harsh words had been said, we'd ended the call with our usual "I love you." Here was someone else, someone who still had a mom, saying she hated her, and ... well ... that was not something I was okay with hearing.

When I didn't think I could make it any longer, I called my brother, hoping to commiserate with him in our shared sorrow. Allen, however, had fostered a military mentality that clashed with my more sentimental nature. He was a soldier at heart. "Pull up your bootstraps, Lauren," he told me. "Keep moving forward."

Allen always seemed so tough. I was trying my best to be tough like him, but inside, I was coming unraveled. Increasingly, I didn't want anyone's help. I didn't need anyone's help. I've got this, I would tell people who tried to offer their support. I did desperately need people, but I pushed them away.

More than that, I found myself drifting further and further away from God, just as I needed Him most. Always before, when things seemed tough in the Sisler household, I was the one who would tell my parents or my brother that things were going to get better. We just had to trust God. But in my darkest days, I found myself struggling to know God myself and to understand how an all-powerful God could let something like this happen to good people like our family.

No one said what I really needed to hear: *Lauren, your feelings are your responsibility. This is your story, and it sucks sometimes. If you wait for someone else to fix your trauma, you will be a victim for the rest of your life.*

It's okay. I probably wouldn't have listened anyway.

Rutgers ended for the year, and Justin drove me back to Roanoke to spend the summer with Aunt Linda and Uncle Mike.

While school has a defined timeline, pain does not.

As a grief-stricken 18-year-old who had already been on my own for a year at an out-of-state college, living in someone else's home that summer proved tough for me. I had a hard time coming under my surrogate parents' authority, even though they were my aunt and uncle whom I had known for years and loved deeply.

My aunt looks a lot like my mom, and her fun-loving personality felt familiar. Most of the time, she was great. Uncle Mike, though, was much different than my dad. He set a curfew for me while I was vacationing with them at the beach, a parental move that I didn't like. Granted, it was a generous curfew of 2:00 a.m., but as far as I was concerned, that wasn't the point. My parents had set a curfew for me, too, but they always let me bend it as long as I would call and check in with them. I was unhappy, and I let Uncle Mike know it.

Aunt Linda laid ground rules, too. She wanted me to clean my room, and not just to my own satisfaction but up to and beyond her more exacting standards. I didn't like that either. It's not that I minded having a clean room. I just struggled with two people other than my mom and dad telling me what to do. It didn't feel right. But then, nothing felt right that summer.

Everything had been thrown off-kilter ever since March 24th.

20

Rumors Abound

ON MONDAY, JUNE 16, THE OFFICE OF THE CHIEF MEDICAL EX-
aminer called Aunt Linda with the news that the toxicology reports
on my parents had arrived from the lab. My aunt insisted I ride
with her to pick them up. We drove to the office in near silence.

The temperature hovered near 90° F that day, and Virginia's high hu-
midity turned the car from just plain hot to sticky-southern hot. Even with
the frigid air blasting out of the vents in the dashboard, it would still feel
stifling to most people but not to me. I was cold, cold all the way through
to my bones.

When we arrived at the medical examiner's office, Aunt Linda put the
car into park and turned to face me. "Do you want to go in?"

"No." I didn't elaborate on my reasons.

Aunt Linda left the car running for me while she ventured into the
examiner's office to collect the reports. I stared blankly out the passenger
window. Before long, she emerged with a manila envelope in hand. When
she climbed back in the car, I could see that the envelope had been opened.
My aunt had read whatever was inside, and she didn't seem surprised.

"Do you want to read these?" Linda handed me the envelope. I
dropped it on the floorboard between my feet without saying a word or
taking a single look inside. Aunt Linda nodded, put the car in reverse, and
drove home.

At the time, I figured that whatever secrets it revealed about my mom
and dad were better left hidden. As far as I was concerned, I now held my
parents' legacy in my hands. And I was going to protect their legacy at all
costs.

It would be another 10 years before I opened that envelope.

Despite my best efforts to enshrine my parents' memories, information—or maybe just rumors—had already begun to leak out. The week my parents died, local journalists started hounding us for information. We received phone calls from the *Roanoke Times* and nearby TV stations, asking for more details. Calls were coming in at my aunt and uncle's house, my grandparents' place, and our home in Giles.

After ignoring several attempts, Allen finally decided to give them their story, detailing what little bit he knew about how they died and focusing on why they were loved by so many.

Using Allen's interview, the *Roanoke Times* published an article titled "Children Mourn Loss of Both Parents." The opening pull quote read, "Lesley and Butch Sisler were both taking pain medication for back problems and may have died from overdoses of medication."

The rest of the article was mostly positive. It quoted my brother as saying that Mom's sausage gravy was "the deal." And it related how much my parents enjoyed themselves when I invited friends over to jump off the rope swing into the New River. The article concluded with Allen's comment that "[t]hey were better off staying together. One would have been miserable without the other one." He was right, I thought. If Mom had to go, it was better that Dad went with her.

I clipped the piece from the newspaper to tuck away with my other treasured mementos. Somehow, though, I missed the entire section that said, "Because of the circumstances surrounding their deaths, rumors have circulated about what happened."

Even if I could selectively read the newspaper, I couldn't miss the talk that swirled around Giles County that summer. My parents were buying or selling illegal drugs, some people said. Others came up with crazier ideas. Probably the most preposterous rumor—and the most hurtful—was that my dad had murdered my mom and then committed suicide himself.

The comments from outsiders not only filled me with anger, but they made me question things I didn't want to consider. I knew my dad would never hurt my mom, but the suicide story touched a nerve. Was it possible that Dad had been so distressed by Mom's death that he decided to end things on his own?

For a long time, I returned to the *what-ifs* surrounding Dad's death. *What if* he really was into illegal drug trades? *What if* my dad really did take his own life?

What-if questions can torture you.

Insurance-related investigators answered that final question for me later in the summer. Dad had not taken his life. His death was ruled accidental, and his insurance disbursement was split equally between Allen and me.

The details about the insurance money gave me my first tangible clue that God had not, in fact, abandoned me. Had my father died first, his insurance money would have gone to my mom. When she died, it would have gone to her estate where it would have been sunk into the massive pit of their debts. That's what happened to my mom's small life insurance policy. It was only $10,000, but neither Allen nor I ever saw a penny of it. Since she died first, however, we each received a financial settlement that helped out.

Discovering the depths of their debt had been rough. I knew, of course, that my parents had financial problems. I just didn't know how desperate their circumstances had become. Aunt Linda spent months sorting through reams of Mom and Dad's financial documents. She learned that their finances had gone further off the rails than anyone knew.

According to what my aunt found, their descent into financial chaos had started slowly and then spiraled out of control. The dream house in the country had cost much more than my parents had originally budgeted. Their contractor wasn't as good as they'd thought, and the power company charged far above what they had first projected to run lines that far off the main road.

Then, Mom and Dad had gotten a high-interest, 15-year mortgage that demanded costly monthly payments. When they couldn't make those payments, my parents took out a second mortgage.

On top of that, my mom had been forced to quit her part-time job due to her diagnosis of degenerative disc disease. At almost the same time, the hospital where Dad worked went through a reorganization that resulted in everyone with his title taking a major pay cut. And of course, there had been the big toys my dad loved, my gymnastics expenses, and my mom's pretty household furnishings. It all formed a perfect storm that hit my family at the worst possible time.

I discovered Mom's car had already been repossessed before she died, and Dad's car was about to go. My parents had also borrowed $23,000 from Gramps to make mortgage payments—payments that weren't always sent to the mortgage company. The dream house was slated for foreclosure, and my parents were desperately trying to sell it before that happened. Mom had never even paid Grandma for the cell phone she bought me when the credit card with my name on it didn't work. Mom couldn't pay. She didn't have the money.

Even my last Christmas gifts had all been purchased on a credit card that Mom opened in my name without telling me. I only discovered the card's existence when the charges went to collections.

As bad as my parents' finances were, I had no inkling of what was coming next until Aunt Linda told me. *The entire estate would be sold at public auction to pay my parents' debts.* Not just the house, Aunt Linda assured me, but all our belongings, too. We couldn't even return to the property to collect anything beyond photographs and sentimental objects with no monetary value.

I vividly remember the day the auction company's truck pulled up at the house. Three men and a woman got out. They entered our house, boxed up all our belongings, and carried them away to be stored, valued, priced, and auctioned off to strangers—complete strangers with no attachment to all these cherished belongings. They even boxed up my mom and dad's clothes.

Watching the movers carry all of my family's personal items from the house drove me further down my pit of depression, even though I thought I was already at the bottom. I comforted myself in the knowledge that I would be back at Rutgers before the estate auction in the fall.

One good thing did happen that summer: I bought a BMW with $24,000 of my dad's insurance money. It was a huge splurge for someone in my circumstances and one that both Aunt Linda and Chrystal Chollet-Norton worried about. But I told myself that the car was a gift from my father, the only person I knew who had loved cars as much as I did. I was smart with the remaining money and deposited it in a money market where it could accrue interest.

The day my parents died, I—a girl who had never even written a check or had more than $50 to my name—became financially independent. Yes, I received a few donations, and my aunt would often buy me things I needed. At no point, however, did my aunt and uncle deposit money into my account or even offer me a loan. I pride myself on that. Aside from the BMW, I remained frugal with what I had.

Newport couple died less than 5 hours apart last week

Children mourn loss of both parents

Lesley and Butch Sisler were both taking pain medication for back problems and may have died from overdoses of medication.

By GREG ESPOSITO
THE ROANOKE TIMES

Lesley and Butch Sisler were always excited to have guests over. Their daughter used to invite friends to their Newport home to jump from a rope swing into the New River. When their son went deer hunting with friends in the early morning hours, his mom made sure there was a big country breakfast waiting for them.

"Sausage gravy was the deal," Allen Sisler said of his mother's breakfasts. "She'd cook it for the masses."

But Allen Sisler, a Navy parachute rigger stationed in Norfolk, and Lauren Sisler, a freshman at Rutgers University, were miles away when they heard that their parents had died less than five hours apart early March 24.

Allen Sisler had spoken with both of his parents the night of March 23. His dad had been suffering with the flu, but other than that the couple were in good spirits. Lesley Sisler, 45, was excited because her son was planning to come home this weekend to visit.

According to the Giles County Sheriff's Office, Butch Sisler awoke about 1 a.m. March 24 and found his wife lying on the porch. He called for help; rescue crews arrived to find her dead. After spending the next few hours at the hospital, Butch Sisler returned home. Someone from the ambulance service called the house to see how he was doing. He collapsed after answering the phone, and for the second time that morning an ambulance rushed to the couple's home on Spruce Run Road. Butch Sisler was pronounced dead at the scene. He was 52.

Both Lesley and Butch Sisler were taking pain medication for back problems, Sgt. Mark Gordon said the sheriff's office isn't investigating either death as suspicious. He said both deaths were likely caused by overdoses of medication but won't know until toxicology reports come back.

Because of the circumstances of their deaths, rumors have circulated about what happened. Allen Sisler is sure of one thing about his father's death.

"There's no way it would've been intentional," he said.

Butch Sisler lost his father when he was 25 years old, and he told friends that he wouldn't wish the experience on anybody. Allen Sisler knows that his father, a Navy veteran who served in Grenada, would never intentionally put his son through the same thing.

Married for 22 years, the Sislers met at Jumbo's Pizza in Roanoke. Shortly after they married, Allen was born and the family moved to Guantanamo Bay, Cuba, where Butch was a Navy diver.

After five years in Cuba that included the birth of their daughter, Butch Sisler left the Navy. The family returned to Roanoke, where Butch and Lesley had both grown up. Allen was introduced to his father's passions: hunting, NASCAR and football. He shot his first gun when he was 5 and was deer hunting by 8. Lauren took up gymnastics at a young age and is a member of the Rutgers gymnastics team.

The family moved to Giles County about six years ago. Allen and his friends hunted nearby and the house often served as a meeting place before and after hunts. Camouflage clothes would pile up in the kitchen and hunters who forgot to take their boots off would track mud inside.

"This ain't gonna turn into no hunting lodge" was a frequent refrain from Lesley Sisler during hunting season. But she would still accommodate the hunters by cooking her pot roast or famous "nuclear cheese dip."

Allen Sisler will return to Norfolk in a week. He doesn't expect to be sent to the Persian Gulf. He said his parents were ecstatic when he returned from duty aboard the USS Roosevelt a year ago after serving in military operations against the Taliban — it meant he could visit frequently. He bought his father tickets to the Virginia 500 for his birthday. The race is in Martinsville in April, and he had planned to come home and attend with his dad. Although he would have liked to have gone to the race with his father, Allen Sisler takes some solace in the fact that his parents died the same day.

"They were better off staying together," he said. "One would've been miserable living without the other one."

Greg Esposito can be reached at 381-1675 or greg.esposito@roanoke.com.

The article that appeared in The Roanoke Times
a week after my parents' death

21

Coming Back to Life

THAT FALL, ALLEN SAVED OUR FAMILY'S HOME. HE DIDN'T DO IT alone, of course.

Our neighbors, friends, and classmates had raised about $3,000 to help us buy back the personal items we wanted at the auction. Most of the project was headed up by Mrs. Ann Wheeler, a teacher who had known Allen and me in school.

I appreciated their help, but I refused to go to the auction. I knew I couldn't handle it emotionally, and I trusted Allen, my tougher-than-nails-won't-lose-his-composure-for-anything brother, to bring back what I might want. Sure enough, he brought me back several items that had sentimental value.

He also purchased the house.

Allen had a good friend whose mom worked as a loan officer at the bank. Together, Allen, his friend, and her mom put together a proposal to buy back our home. He called me with the news that his offer had been accepted.

I didn't care.

"I'm glad for you, Allen," I said. "But I don't want to go back in that house. I couldn't stand seeing the floor where they found Dad's body or the bathroom where Mom died."

He understood, I think.

Grief is a funny thing. The same tragedy can strike two different people in totally different ways. I could have gone the rest of my life without stepping a foot past the door of the house on Boars Head Trail. That house had nothing good left for me. Allen, however, wanted to hold onto the place that Mom and Dad had loved so much. For him, the house was an anchor, and for his sake, I was glad he could buy it back.

As far as I was concerned, genuine relief from the daily ache of life without my parents lay in New Jersey, not at the end of the road in rural Virginia. The Rutgers gymnastics team became my new day-to-day family.

They proved it that October when my birthday rolled around—the first birthday since my parents had passed away. I had been dreading it for weeks. How could I celebrate when the people who loved me most were gone?

It turns out that I shouldn't have worried. As always, my team was in my corner.

Kathy Galli, our athletic trainer, hosted a birthday party for me at her house. The entire team pitched in to buy me gifts and made the day as special as possible. The NCAA usually frowns on those kinds of events, but Kathy got special permission due to the circumstances. I have never forgotten her gesture.

In our gymnastics family, as with every family, real love wasn't just about parties and gifts. Love also meant we had to have hard conversations and receive caring discipline. My Rutgers family didn't disappoint me there either.

It was clear to everyone that I wasn't handling my situation well. I poured my entire self into gymnastics, smiled little, and discussed my parents less. The Lauren on their team that fall was much different than the giddy girl who had competed at her first collegiate competition just a few months earlier.

I learned one truth about grief very quickly—life doesn't stop. Everyday hardships keep on coming without waiting for you to recover from your trauma. Early in my sophomore year, I continued to struggle with the effects of the back injuries I'd sustained as a high school gymnast. Then, I compounded those by fracturing my femur.

I didn't care.

I didn't even tell anybody I was hurt. I just dragged a bum leg around the Rutgers campus. Kathy was ready to wring my neck, but I didn't care about that, either. Finally, she insisted I get an MRI, which revealed a giant hole in my bone. When the coaches found out, I was forced to sit on the sidelines until my leg healed. If that fracture turned into a break, the doctor told me, the bone shards could hit an artery, and I would die almost immediately.

I still didn't care.

My biggest fear wasn't death. I had faced that already when death came and stole both my parents, and I survived. My biggest fear was that I would be a disappointment. I felt like the only people I had left to fight for were my teammates, and I worried that Chrystal and the whole Rutgers athletic department would think I was a wasted scholarship. I wanted people to believe I belonged, not that I was a has-been gymnast who had too many problems to benefit the team. So I kept pushing through the pain of my injuries, thereby putting myself—and everyone around me—in greater and greater peril.

It wasn't just my athletic skills that took a tumble that fall. My academic life was falling apart, too. Once an A/B honor roll student, Cs and Ds became my new normal. I had never seen an F on a paper in my life—until that semester. I cried myself to sleep every night about my grades. If tears could raise someone's GPA, I would have been golden, but all the struggling college students who went before me could have attested that my weeping would do me no good. I knew that time with my books was what I needed to have better grades, but I was too distraught to study.

In short, I was a mess.

That semester, Coach Chollet-Norton sat me down for a good talk. My erratic behavior and poor study habits weren't just hurting me, she told me. I was injuring the whole team. The coach knew how desperately I loved and needed my team, so her words cut deep, down to my fractured femur.

"You are spending so much time living in a dream world, Lauren, that you're not facing the reality of what your life is becoming," Coach Chollet-Norton told me. "Here's the deal—you don't keep up your grades; you lose your scholarship. You lose your scholarship; you can't afford to stay in school. You don't stay in school; you don't get a degree, and your chances of finding success become more and more uncertain."

I needed to figure things out, and I needed to do so quickly.

Coach Chollet-Norton had the courage to speak the hard facts that everyone else was too scared to tell me. She had given me the space and freedom to be a mess for a while, but it was time for me to clean up my act. For all of the hard truth she told me, Coach Chollet-Norton was loving, too—like always. She asked me point blank, "What would help you get back on track?"

I didn't know what would help me. I didn't even want to get back on track. I wanted to wallow in grief. I wanted to keep using the dramatic cry "but my parents *died*" as a way of shirking my obligations. Chrystal didn't let me do any of that. She insisted I take responsibility for myself and my role on the team. She was right. My parents couldn't come back to life, but I could, and I needed to.

So I did what I had to do. I asked the university for tutors and took advantage of the counseling that Rutgers offered. Getting back into the habit of studying was no easy task, but years of consistent effort in the gym had led to success in gymnastics, so I decided to apply the same consistency in the library and trust that the results would follow.

As I became reinvigorated for life, I felt a spark in my soul. I dove back into my faith and got involved in Athletes in Action, a Christian group similar to the Fellowship of Christian Athletes. That semester, I began to let God carry me through the hard times instead of asking Him why He had left me to face them all alone. I started to really live the message of the "Footprints" poem, not just recite it.

The more I leaned into my faith, the more I realized how present God had been in the last seven months. I had closed my eyes the night of my parents' deaths and chosen to stay in my darkness. I didn't realize that He was there the whole time, offering me light. I began to feel and truly believe that God hadn't abandoned me.

Just as God kept pursuing me, so did my family in Virginia. Aunt Linda called and sent packages regularly, and Justin burned up the roads between Roanoke and Rutgers. He came to see me so often, in fact, that the gymnastics team eventually dubbed him our unofficial mascot.

Even then, I knew that it was the Rutgers gymnastics team and my mom's family that were holding me together. If God had allowed my original plan of going to the Air Force Academy—a school 1,500 miles from my family in Virginia—I would never have had the kind of support I needed. That's how I learned that God had a plan to carry me before I even knew I needed help walking.

With support from Aunt Linda, Chrystal, Kathy, and my teammates, I slowly began to return to life. You know when you lose feeling in your foot? Maybe you sat too long in one position and didn't have good blood flow. Before you realize what's happened, your foot has become useless. When you try to stand up, your foot is unresponsive, and you have to catch yourself from falling. It brings discomfort, but you shake your foot and move around to get your blood flowing. The numbness turns to tingling needles. You hate the process, but you know it's good and necessary; your body is returning to its proper state.

That's what was happening to me on a grand scale. I was shaking off my debilitating grief and letting life once again flow through my veins. My faith re-awakened, my grades crept up, and I even laughed occasionally.

Although my efforts led to massive progress, some things just couldn't come back to the way they were.

I finally had to admit that the rigors of pre-medical coursework followed by four years of med school and a residence in sports medicine would be more than I could manage. Even for people who don't have a major crisis or financial concerns, becoming a doctor is a daunting challenge. To keep pursuing that career would mean destroying my fragile emotional health, which I was working so diligently to rebuild. I needed a new major and a new life plan.

A change of career plans meant I would need to confess my failure as a pre-medical major to Aunt Linda and Uncle Mike, my surrogate parents who were both accomplished medical professionals themselves. I decided to wait and tell them in person over the holidays. I used the time leading up to Christmas to try to work up the nerve.

Though it had been nine months since my parents had both died on the same night, this marked the first holiday season without them. Some of my fondest memories with my parents centered around Thanksgiving and Christmas—the delicious dinners, the tasteful decorating, and the piles of gifts. I knew this year would be an emotional and painful celebration.

After my last exam ended at Rutgers around 6:00 p.m., I hopped into my BMW and drove the eight-hour stretch down Interstate 81 so I could maximize the time with my family for Christmas. Even though I felt nervous about celebrating without my parents, as soon as I walked in the front door, I knew I wouldn't be disappointed.

My aunt outdid herself, and it all came from her loving heart. Aunt Linda knew my parents liked to buy Allen and me lots of gifts at Christmas, so she went all out and bought more than I'd ever gotten from my parents. Even at age 19, I knew my aunt was overcompensating, but I didn't try to stop her. It was good to feel loved so warmly and generously.

Aunt Linda did everything she could to keep our family traditions intact and give me the kind of Christmas I had always known and loved with Mom and Dad. We baked Nanny's cookies, fixed our favorite Christmas snacks, and indulged in the enduring comedy of *National Lampoon's Christmas Vacation* on Christmas Eve and *A Christmas Story* on Christmas Day. My aunt would continue these traditions for me until she knew I was ready to start making new memories.

I began to learn that when you lose something precious, it feels like a rock has been taken out of the river. The rock once filled a space, and for a split second, there's nothing there to take its place. Then, the river comes rushing in to fill that space where the rock sat. If my parents had been my rock, surely Aunt Linda was the river who helped fill the space their absence created.

Even though I had a wonderful holiday with my family, I needed to get back to New Jersey by the first weekend after New Year's when gymnastics practice resumed. I left Virginia before the dorms opened back up at Rutgers, so I bunked in for a few days with an upperclassman who lived off campus. Her name was Laura Iepson, and she had lost her brother in a car accident the previous year. We connected with each other deeply over our shared grief, and it was an odd kind of comfort to have a break from the glittering lights and the gifts to be with someone who understood the opposing emotions of loss and celebration.

Only at Laura's house—500 miles away from southern Virginia—did I finally build up my courage to discuss my changing plans with Uncle Mike and Aunt Linda. From the kitchen of my host's house, I called "home" to Virginia. Aunt Linda answered, and I asked her to get Uncle Mike to pick up the extension.

With both of them on the phone, I nervously confessed that I didn't think I wanted to pursue a career in medicine anymore. I admitted that I was struggling with my grades; I wasn't passionate about becoming a doctor. And to get to the heart of the matter, I didn't think I was cut out for that profession.

"I just don't want to tape feet for the rest of my life," I told them. To my relief, they seemed to understand.

"It's okay to change direction, Lauren," my uncle said. Waves of relief washed over me when he told me that. "It's probably for the best that you go ahead and make this change now," he added.

Uncle Mike recommended I take some personality and skills tests to discover what I had a natural aptitude for. Being Uncle Mike, he also calculated how many As I would have to earn to bring up my sagging GPA to something respectable. His calculations boggled my mind, but I was determined to accomplish the task.

We had a good talk that night, and when I hung up the phone, I felt like a weight had lifted. Finally, I could move with confidence in a different direction, and I didn't have to be afraid of disappointing anyone.

I met with my academic advisor to discuss my options, and I took a few personality and assessment tests to help me decide what career goal might fit me best. I had my options narrowed down, but I really have Dawn Giel, one of my closest teammates, to thank for my career. Dawn majored in communication, and she had plans to be a sports reporter. One day at lunch, she said to me, "Laurie, I think you would be great at sports broadcasting. You've got the personality for it, and it would be fun to pursue this career together!"

Dawn gave me the push I needed. I decided that communication was the major for me. After all, I love to talk. Oh boy, do I love to talk! Like my dad, I can strike up a conversation with just about anybody. But it isn't just the talking that I enjoy. It's talking to people so I can make a difference in their lives. Maybe I got that part from Mom. So, I decided to pursue a career in broadcasting—a place where I had the power to influence and impact people in their day-to-day lives.

Even as life continued around me and my goals changed, the memory of my parents remained consistent. They were never far from my mind, and thankfully, other people didn't forget them either. Later in my sophomore year, the gymnastics team planted a weeping cherry tree in front of the gym where we trained. It was both to honor my parents and to memorialize Laura Iepson's brother.

At the year-end banquet, my team also presented me with a glass plaque with both my parents' names engraved on it, a beautiful gift that I treasure to this day. Even though my parents' time of influence was cut short, that plaque from my teammates helped me see that Mom and Dad were still part of my Rutgers journey.

Throughout the remainder of my time in college, I stayed dedicated to both my gymnastics and scholarly goals, making slow but continual progress. Upon entering my junior year, I was ready to leave my mark at Rutgers.

Determination alone, however, didn't help me make the cut. While I was able to stay reasonably healthy, I just couldn't quite crack the competition lineup. Devastated and guilt stricken—a horrible feeling I knew all too well—I believed that I had let the team and coaches down for yet another year. I was an upperclassman at this point. I was supposed to be leading my team and helping to earn those high scores at competitions. I should have been setting the example for the younger girls, and I was not ... but they thought I was.

My teammates voted me co-captain for the 2005–2006 season. Even though I didn't have the success I wanted in the gym, the girls saw my tenacity, and they believed that was more important than the medals I did not have. They said I had been an inspiration and role model to my team members. It was an honor to be looked at by others as a leader, especially when I didn't think I was.

With the title of co-captain beside my name and only one more year of gymnastics before the end of my college career, I was going to step up to the plate and make my senior year the most successful and memorable season of my life. Even though my parents wouldn't be there to see it, I was going to be great, the kind of great they always saw in me.

Once again, though, I was met with challenges. I tore two ligaments in my ankle while training a new tumbling pass, just as I was looking ahead to my senior year. Ever determined, I made gymnastics my number one priority during my summer break and told myself that no injury was going to stop me. I spent hours upon hours in the gym getting back the skills I once had. As a captain, I felt I had a responsibility to uphold.

When the fall semester welcomed me back to campus, all my hard work finally paid off. That year, I was back to training on all four events with a significant spot in lineups on two, the bars and the floor.

It was a memorable season! I was selected as the lead-off competitor on both bars and floor, an honor typically reserved for the most consistent gymnast in the lineup—not always the flashiest or most skilled, just the most consistent. That was me. I was the tone-setter. It fit well with the entire theme of my senior year. I had started setting the tone for better days ahead and a brighter future.

For some reason, I chose "NFL on Fox" as the theme music for my final floor routines. I did football-related signals—touchdown, personal foul, facemask, and at the end, I struck the Heisman pose. It turned out to be a bit of a prophetic routine—football was in my future. Many years later, when I was reporting on football games from the sidelines for ESPN, I came to appreciate God's sense of humor. He knew where He was carrying me even when it didn't make sense to me at the time.

Swinging bars at one of my final gymnastics competitions for Rutgers in 2006

Rutgers Gymnastics senior portraits after being voted team captain

I'm center-left in the middle row.

Rutgers Gymnastics banquet with Rutgers head coach Chrystal Chollet-Norton and team athletic trainer Kathy Galli (Spring 2006)

Back at Rutgers with Chrystal and Kathy 16 years later

I owe my transition from sports medicine to sports broadcasting to Dawn Giel. She lit the flame and stuck by my side to watch it catch fire.

A special bond was shared with Laura Iepson over grief and loss.

Soaking up Rutgers life with my cousins, Justin (right) and Jason (behind)

I began to fall in love with all the new memories that Aunt Linda and Uncle Mike created for our family at Christmas.
(Photo by Stephanie Klein-Davis/Roanoke Times)

22

Torn Between Telling the Truth and Keeping Secrets

BY THE TIME I WOUND UP MY GYMNASTICS CAREER AT RUTGERS, the rumors on campus surrounding my parents' deaths had mostly come to a halt, but I remained quick to defend Mom and Dad anytime their names came up. For a while, the rumors were weeds that overtook everything, and I was the repellent that dried them up so that they couldn't spread further. Thankfully, as graduation approached, only an occasional weed sprouted its head for me to stamp out.

Telling the story of my mom's death was easy enough. Early on, someone—I don't remember who—had used the words *respiratory failure*. I latched onto them. As for my dad, he had landed himself in the hospital just a few months before he passed away, and he had struggled with heart issues for some time.

When people asked me, "What happened to your parents?" I had a believable story ready to trot out for them: "My mom died of respiratory failure, and my dad couldn't live without her. He had cardiovascular problems already, and he died of a heart attack just five hours after my mom passed away."

The longer I told the story, the easier it was to tell. Since I refused to read the toxicology reports or any other documentation related to my parents' passing, I didn't know that my story *wasn't* true. I didn't want to know if it was. And everyone seemed to believe me. Even Kathy, our team's onsite medical professional, didn't look surprised by what I told her. If an expert thought it was plausible, then I knew I had a story I could stick with.

Only occasionally did I crack under the growing mountain of evidence about what really happened to Mom and Dad. One of those times was when I got nominated for the Wilma Rudolph Award, an honor given to a Division 1 student athlete who maintained good academic standing while demonstrating perseverance.

All the nominees had to write an essay, and academic advisors across the country judged the entries. I wrote everything except the first paragraph of my essay; something kept me from writing my rehearsed tale of their deaths. Maybe it was that it seemed disrespectful to tell the story in light of such a humbling honor, or maybe my faith in the story finally flagged.

Whatever the case, I couldn't bear to tell my own explanation one more time, but I just couldn't bring myself to write the truth about how my parents died either. Aunt Linda helped me out and crafted the first paragraph for me.

> Shortly before I started writing this, I received an article from my Aunt Linda that had recently been front page news in the newspaper in my hometown. Just below the large print of *The Roanoke Times* read, "Prescription drug death toll rising, again" in bold letters. I wasn't sure I was ready to read the article. But three years have almost passed since the day my life changed forever. It was time for me to tear down this wall that I have kept up for so long and to take a look at something that has greatly affected my life as well as those around me.

I went on to read the article which also said, "The death toll from prescription drug abuse in Western Virginia is on the rise."

I continued with my essay.

> And sadly, the statistics show for the year of 2005, Western Virginia is nearing another all-time high record. My parents are among the statistics they presented in the article for the year 2003. They both fell victim to this devastating addiction which ultimately succumbed to their untimely deaths just a few hours apart from each other.

Was I really admitting this in front of these people? I was, and I continued with the script Linda had prepared for me to read. "On that day, my life and the lives of my brother, Allen, my grandparents, aunts, uncles, numerous cousins, and countless loving friends were left with many questions, little answers, and a substantial amount of heartbreak and pain."

Aunt Linda was right, of course. It was time for me to tear down the wall I had kept up for so long. It was time for me to look at the way addiction had ravaged my family ... but I just couldn't do that. Not yet. Maybe I would not ever stare it straight on. For the time, all I could do was peek around the door like a scared child, but also like a child, each peek made me feel a little braver.

Growing up, I had never precisely understood what addiction was. Stories of addicts usually told of severely dysfunctional people, something Mom and Dad were not. They were both warm and affectionate parents who provided me and my brother with a loving home. Something like addiction just couldn't have had a hold on my parents, two of the strongest people I knew. I couldn't even use the words "addiction" or "overdose" in the same sentence with my parents' names. It was unfathomable!

However, as more and more facts about Mom and Dad's addictions emerged, I found it harder and harder to hold on to my comforting story about respiratory failure and a sympathetic heart attack. And yes, despite my efforts to remain blissfully ignorant, new information about their problems was coming to light all the time.

My dad's collapse the Thanksgiving before he died hadn't been a mix-up with his medications. He had overdosed. That Thanksgiving Day, while Justin and I sat in the hospital waiting room, Dad had confessed to my mom that he'd looked up on the internet how to get the biggest high possible from a fentanyl patch.

He'd learned that if you freeze a patch, the fentanyl will turn into a gel. Suck out the gel, and you'll fly high as a kite, leaving your worries on the ground and spending a few hours on Cloud 9. Of course, you can also go into respiratory failure and die, which is what he nearly did. Just four months later, that's exactly what happened to my mother.

On the night my parents died, police discovered empty medicine bottles with prescriptions for 348 OxyContin pills, 60 oxycodone pills, 30 Lorcet-Plus tablets, and 52 Mepergan Fortis tablets. In other words, Mom and Dad had been prescribed a total of 490 pills of various opioid medications between January 8 and March 4, 2003. They had filled every prescription and nearly emptied every bottle.

Nearly all of the narcotic medication was prescribed to my mom, but clearly, my dad had been helping himself to her stash. He did have a few narcotic prescriptions of his own, though, including (shockingly!) one pre-scribed to him just three weeks after his near-fatal overdose at Thanksgiv-ing.

Later, I learned that the EMTs had dislodged part of a fentanyl patch from the back of my mom's throat during their attempts to resuscitate her. Every single thing about my parents' deaths spelled *addict*. But I couldn't use that word, not even when the full truth came out.

Although the medical team at the hospital had recorded my dad's col-lapse in November 2002 as an overdose—and even sent him for a psych evaluation and rehabilitation at St. Albans—Mom and Dad's pain manage-ment doctor continued to flood them with prescription medications, enough to keep both her and Dad feeling numb in the middle of all their emotional and physical pain.

Of course, the most damning evidence of all lay in the toxicology re-ports, which I still refused to read. Had I opened them, I would have known that on the night Mom and Dad died, they each had ingested enough fentanyl to kill them twice over.

Their behaviors—the overspending, the secrecy, the financial disar-ray, the missed work—pointed to a serious addiction problem. To anyone with all the information, the truth was obvious: my parents were full-blown drug addicts with access to a prescriber who was behaving more like a drug supplier than a medical doctor.

The conversation surrounding narcotics in America was much differ-ent at the turn of the century than it is today.

In 1980, a non-research-based article was published saying that opi-oids had a 0.03 percent chance of becoming addictive. In the 1990s, there was a huge push from the federal government, physician associations, the Veterans Administration, and the American Pain Society to give more at-tention to pain management. As a result, the Drug Enforcement Agency promised less regulation over opioids in 2000.[1]

The medical community even called it inhumane not to prescribe opi-oids when people were in pain, and patients could sue if they didn't get the

---

[1] Jones, Mark R, Omar Viswanath, Jacquelin Peck, Alan D Kaye, Jatinder S Gill, and Thomas T Simopoulos. "A Brief History of the Opioid Epidemic and Strategies for Pain Medi-cine." Pain and therapy, June 2018. https://www.ncbi.nlm.nih.gov/pmc/arti-cles/PMC5993682/.

treatment. From 1997–2002, OxyContin prescriptions increased from 670,000 to 6.2 million and continued to climb throughout the 2000s.[2]

Both of my parents waged a secret war with addiction, their means to help them cope with their chronic pain and depression. While they lost battle after battle to the pills and patches, they refused to add any numbers to their army. No one in our family was privy to their struggle; no one knew the extent of their pain. I believe they were shielding us and everyone around them from something they felt was too shameful to disclose, protecting us from their overwhelming enemy and mounting the losses in silence.

But I had a problem, too: I was just as shackled by shame as Mom and Dad were. Just like they were too embarrassed to ask for help, so was I. Just like they hid their secrets from the world, so did I.

I didn't know it then, but I would later learn that our sad or tragic experiences don't have to be defined as sad or tragic. They can also be positive influences and shape us in a healthy way.

At just 22, I simply didn't want to let go of the loving memory of my childhood. My parents were my everything, and they gave me everything I'd ever loved. If I loosened my grip on my explanations for their deaths, would the tragic reality topple down and crush all the goodness of the past?

---

[2] Ibid.

23

Leaving Jersey and Telling Stories

May 17, 2006
Rutgers

AUNT LINDA AND UNCLE MIKE, GRANDMA AND GRAMPS, AND MY childhood gymnastics buddy Kearstin and her mom and stepdad all came to see me graduate with my bachelor's degree in Communication. Just like I promised Uncle Mike, I had brought my GPA up from a 2.5 to a respectable 3.2. Although I was excited about moving from school to a career, college graduation marked yet another milestone that Mom and Dad missed.

That summer, I put my degree to use right away and landed a job as a technical associate at CNBC in Englewood Cliffs, New Jersey, located about 45 miles from the Rutgers campus. Financial news wasn't my calling, but after interning there the summer before, it was a great starting point for me to learn broadcasting from the ground up.

My supervisors gave me a wide range of job duties behind the scenes, but the one I remember most was running the teleprompter for on-air talent. At first, it seemed like a fairly easy job until the studio anchor or reporter would go completely off-script and send me into a panic. I had to make my own judgment calls about where they would go next. It was a new way of getting that shot of adrenaline I loved.

Even though I didn't know much about the stock market or finances, being in that control room taught me about the inner workings of live TV. I learned that every individual has a unique responsibility and plays a critical role. It was a perspective that served me well as I launched into my television career.

Believe it or not, though, I was itching to get back home to Virginia. In the wake of my parents' deaths, I wanted nothing more than to get far away from all the memories, but after graduation, I found myself missing my people. The structure of school and the companionship of my gymnastics team were over, and I needed my family and my childhood friends. With each visit, Virginia grew closer to my heart and once again became home. I was convinced Virginia was where I needed to be.

I discovered for the first time—but not the last—that healing comes in layers. Over the past four years, my broken heart had indeed begun to mend. I was ready to go back to a small Southern town again, no matter how much it reminded me of Mom and Dad. I began to send out resumes to stations across southern Virginia. Every time a new job in the region would pop up on TVJobs.com, I shot them an inquiry. I wanted so badly to be back home.

It happened sooner than I thought. In 2007, a new job as a video photographer and editor opened up at WDBJ7, my hometown station in Roanoke. I applied, interviewed, got an offer, and accepted it in near record time.

That summer, I packed up and left New Jersey. At the time, I felt like I was living the dream—I was leaving the place where I felt alone and going to work at a TV station where everything was familiar and brought back all the good feelings of the past.

When I first arrived, I stayed with Aunt Linda and Uncle Mike in "my" room at their house. It was the perfect arrangement as I settled into my new job and got a few paychecks under my belt, but I quickly looked for another place to live. In my early 20s, I still wanted to hang out with friends and enjoy the social scene. Linda and Mike were thrilled for me as I found a place to rent and took that next step toward adulthood.

I was moving toward independence, but I wouldn't be alone. I searched for a roommate, and I was delighted with whom I found. My childhood best friend, Ellie Augustine, whom I had seen much less frequently than I had wanted since my parents moved us to Giles County, moved in with me, and we picked up where we had left off about a decade earlier.

Not only was my living situation going well, but so was my work life. In my new job, I got to work on "real" news stories, stories that people cared about. That was exactly where I wanted to be, but really, I would have been glad for anything that helped me grow my skills and gain experience with broadcasting. My true interest still lay in sports journalism, but I was thankful to be getting my reps in covering a multitude of news stories, some positive and happy, others dark and sad. I thought I could handle those stories despite my own trauma.

I was wrong.

Once, I went to dinner with my friends, Ashley Richardson and Amanda Patterson, at the Buffalo Wild Wings just up the road from where I lived in Roanoke. Throughout our meal, I watched a heavy-set man at the bar grow increasingly more intoxicated. Soon, he was quite drunk. He got up to leave, and the bartender said, "Hey, let's call you a cab. You don't need to drive right now."

The man didn't agree and began to argue. As the drunk man's belligerent responses grew louder, so did the bartender's concern. Finally, the man walked out the door and stood on the sidewalk in front of the restaurant. He jangled his keys back and forth as if arguing with himself about the wisdom of driving in his condition. Ashley, Amanda, and I went outside with the bartender in hopes of convincing the man to stay put and not drive home.

"I'm good. I'm good," the man kept saying.

With no warning, he stepped backward off the curb and started backpedaling in the air like an old cartoon character. Before we could move, his head hit the cement so hard that we could hear his skull crack. His eyes popped open, and I knew there had to be blood behind his head.

The bartender immediately called the rescue squad, and of course, they whisked him away in an ambulance. I never knew the guy's name, never knew if he made it or not. It all stuck with me for days: the intoxication, the argument, the fall, the blood. I wanted to know what happened. Sometimes, I felt like I *needed* to know. I felt like I was part of that whole event somehow, and it was my right to find out the end of the story.

Of course, seeing that man's fall took me into a dark place. He reminded me of Dad. Both of them were large men. Both liked to drink. Both might have ended their lives because of an addiction they couldn't control. That man's fall opened my eyes a little more to the reality of what substance abuse could do to people.

Many of the stories I covered for the TV station were morbid, too. I had to report on shootings, fatal car accidents, and brutal deaths. At one of our video shoots, I witnessed blood splattered on the curb where a child had been shot. At the scene of a car accident, I saw body bags on the ground. Another time, I had to take photographs of a person with sheets draped over them. It seemed like everywhere I went, death stared me in the face, and I was supposed to stare back and point a camera at it.

It was a bit of a precarious position to be in, but I quickly realized that you can't undo the things that happen to other people. You can only manage your response to them.

That may seem cold, but after spending years shrinking away from the hard truth, I had to accept it as reality. It's what happens. It's part of life, and I knew it, but I didn't want my life to be surrounded by death, by people losing everything.

In that job, I saw up close how the news cycle works, and it's not pretty. We used headlines just to draw viewers' attention with no concern for how they affected the family members of the people involved. The hardest part for me was the invasion of other people's privacy. When you're covering a tough story, you have to put a camera in someone's face and push, push, push until they either give you what you want or tell you to get off their property.

It isn't easy for any news journalist, but for me, it was nearly impossible. I knew all too well what it was like to be hunted down by journalists who wanted to get a story. After my parents died, local journalists hounded Allen, Aunt Linda, and me. If we didn't provide information, they printed whatever they wanted. Our hands were tied.

Now a journalist myself, I was starting to realize how important it was to respect other people's privacy, to realize the emotions present on the other end of the camera. Throughout my career, I have carried a sense of empathy and respect for people in crisis. I try not to get too intrusive, instead letting people speak when they're ready. It has worked in my career and personal relationships. You can encourage other people to share their stories, but you can't force them. If they're not ready, they're not ready.

I wasn't ready. Not ready to push others to their breaking point, and not ready to face my own fears and learn how my parents died. By this time, five years had passed since the night I got that terrible call from my dad. Five years, and I still refused to read the toxicology reports, use the word *addiction* in conversation, or allow anyone to talk about my parents' relationship with prescription drugs in my presence.

One night, at the station in Roanoke, I struck up a conversation with Keith Humphry, one of my colleagues. He had been the star anchor at

WDBJ since I was a child. He knew the story of my parents' deaths and, like many, assumed a lot about what happened. Obviously, he wasn't privy to all the details, but he was aware that prescription drugs were involved. Keith had never said anything to me about it, and maybe it was his respectful silence that I found welcoming.

Over the time that we worked together, I started to trust Keith's insight. One night, with just the two of us in the room, I decided to crack open the door to my personal life and ask Keith for his perspective on things. "There is so much I don't know about my parents' deaths," I told him. "So many unknowns. I hate not having all the answers."

Keith looked at me gently and then said in a soft voice, "Lauren, we're not always going to get answers. We can easily spend more time looking for answers than just focusing on what's right in front of us."

"What is right in front of me now?" I asked him.

"Life."

I didn't understand what Keith meant. His answer frustrated me, but at the same time, I wanted him to tell me more.

"Don't constantly try to find answers from the past," he explained. "Focus forward."

Keith's words were exactly what I needed to hear.

Once more, someone had given me a gift, a sense of direction for where to go next, and a way to handle my grief. This conversation spurred others, and my layers of lies chipped ever so slightly, revealing glimpses of the real me I had hidden underneath. While the circumstances of my past didn't change, my inner self slowly began to transform as God placed people like Keith to walk alongside me for a while.

I put my parents' troubles in an imaginary box, locked it, and stored it on the shelf in my mind. For a long time, I felt guilty—guilty if I told anyone the truth and equally guilty if I didn't. On the one hand, sharing the story of addiction and death felt like I was being a poor steward of Mom and Dad's legacy. They lived full, good, loving lives. Why focus on the tragic ending? But then, when did silence ever help? How could I fall in love with my own story if I couldn't learn to love theirs?

It would be many years before I discovered that I didn't need to feel guilty for categorizing and storing my memories in mental boxes. My therapist explained it like this:

Would you just dump all your stuff in the middle of your house and obsessively look at it every day? Of course not. You store things in drawers, on shelves, or in boxes. You keep your everyday things, like dinnerware or your toothbrush, in easy-to-reach places. Other things, like holiday decorations, you squirrel away in a box because you just put them out once a year. A few precious items you might keep in a locked safe and only remove them when you need them.

It's the same with our memories. Our most precious memories can be stored in mental boxes. At some point, whenever we're ready, we can jump off the couch, grab the box, and tear it open. That only happens when we reach the point where we fear our own stagnation more than we fear our story.

As a young journalist, I was still keeping a lid on all my own personal memory boxes, but I was also beginning to sort through what I could in order to help others in trauma. I wanted to be part of their healing rather than take advantage of them as some journalists did. Soon, I realized that the sports world told better stories than the news did.

A lot of fresh-faced broadcast journalism graduates say they hope to go into sports and wind up news anchors all their lives. Not me. I was more convinced than ever that sports was going to be my focus, and I was going to succeed in it. In sports, we get to talk about celebrations, wins, victories, and accomplishments, giving us a new perspective and inspiration. We can tell these stories with pride and joy instead of worrying about how they hurt others. We focus on the people who play the games, not just the games they play.

Yes, telling other people's stories was what I wanted to do with my life.

24

How I Became a Sports Reporter (and a Dang Good Liar)

D ESPITE POPULAR OPINION, NEWS JOURNALISTS IN SMALL-town markets aren't getting rich quick—or even getting rich at all. I earned a whopping $9.50 an hour in my first TV job. After seeing my parents' financial struggles, I didn't want to repeat their mistakes by living on credit. I knew I needed to earn more money, especially if I was going to fund my love for cars.

And I had definitely inherited Dad's taste for cars. The used BMW that I bought with some of Dad's life insurance money got me through college, but then, it developed maintenance issues. Dawn Giel's dad, who treated me like his own daughter, was a seasoned mechanic, and he worked on that car as needed while I was in school at Rutgers and never charged me a dime. Then came his fatherly advice—sell it and stay away from the cars that cost a fortune to maintain.

Well, I took part of his advice. I sold the BMW ... the second part of his recommendation seemed less necessary. The next summer, I bought a cool, slightly used, sporty Lexus IS350 with a black exterior and interior. To honor my parents, I paid extra for a vanity license plate that read S1SLER.

That car was everything I wanted, but I just needed some way to pay for it. I had already saved thousands upon thousands of dollars by not drinking in college, and other people's bar tabs convinced me that I could either drink my money away or drive it. Without a doubt, I wanted to drive it.

Saving money on alcohol wasn't enough, however, to pay for my new Lexus. I needed a side gig, so I turned to what I knew—dancing. No, not the dancing some women turn to for quick cash, but my kind of dancing, the kind that allows you to be goofy and have fun.

I became a deejay. DJ SIZZLER! A pretty solid name, if you ask me.

My first gig came about thanks to my patronage of Corned Beef & Co., a restaurant and pub in downtown Roanoke. I loved going there on the weekends. Every Friday night, I was the first one on the dance floor and the last one to leave. After a while, I became good friends with the deejay — DJ the Deejay. DJ offered me an opportunity to work for him.

It was a natural fit for me, a photographer and news editor during the weekdays and deejay at night and on the weekends. I deejayed at Corned Beef & Co. and Buffalo Wild Wings as well as at weddings, parties, and even that Holiday Inn off Starkey Road.

I always kept the music going past the last call, usually not leaving until around 2:30 a.m. Then, I'd return the equipment to DJ's house and go home to crash on my bed around 3 a.m. for what became a solid power nap. Then, my alarm would wake me up at 5 a.m. to get ready for work, which started at 6 a.m. It was a pretty crazy schedule!

I made it work for two years before I landed my next full-time job in broadcasting.

Getting a job in TV journalism is a lot like being recruited for athletics in college. You put together a resume reel, send it all over the country, and hope someone likes you enough to take a chance on you.

Before I could make my big move in sports journalism, I had to find ways to gain some experience. First, WDBJ gave me opportunities to work as a grip for Friday night football games. Basically, that means I served as a spotter or statistician for the photographer shooting the highlights.

Back at the TV station, I helped write a script for the sports anchor to read over the highlights during the show. Eventually, I was the one shooting the game highlights.

Finally, I worked up the courage to ask if I could report on a game. Happily, the guys in the sports department—Mike Stevens, Travis Wells, Grant Kittelson, and Chris Miles—gave me a shot. And that's all I needed, someone to believe in me as much as I believed in myself. They all did. One game led to two, and then there were a few, giving me enough footage to put together a "sports reel," one that was decent enough to send to prospective stations.

So there I was, once again labeling videos of myself and sending them off with a little prayer that whoever watched it would like me. I would have loved to transition into a sports role in Roanoke and not move away, but nothing became available.

Before long, I got a call from WTAP in Parkersburg, West Virginia. They needed a sports reporter and a weekend sports anchor. Would I travel in for an interview?

Parkersburg is a tiny town, barely getting its own dot on the map. The TV station wasn't big either. In the TV world, stations get assigned a DMA, or designated market area, which is a number based on the size of their viewership. For example, New York is number 1. Roanoke is around 70. Parkersburg is designated at 194 out of 210 total media markets. The TV market there was very, very small—the perfect place for a new on-air broadcaster to learn the ropes. Making your mistakes in front of as few people as possible is critical to succeeding in this field.

And make mistakes I did. But that's where I got my reps. That's where I learned more about sports—every sport, not just football, basketball, and baseball, but also high school tennis, volleyball, and soccer. It was my first on-air sports reporting job, and it was a tremendous experience for me, one I felt lucky to have.

Because I didn't have the foundation or mentorship that many people in my business utilize, I had to embrace the challenge and see it through to the end. I didn't think twice before taking the plunge to Parkersburg.

Sports reporting is mostly a man's job, so it was a little risky to take on that kind of work as a woman. Would I be able to move up from Parkersburg? Would anyone choose to hire me if a man applied for the same job? But I have always been a risk taker. You don't get to be a top-level gymnast by playing it safe, and that up-for-a-challenge attitude bled over into my career.

A lot of athletes and other sports-related professionals grow up with a hero, somebody they want to emulate. Since I saw so few women on TV reporting about sports, I didn't have anyone to idolize. At the time, sideline reporter Erin Andrews was the best-known woman in sports journalism, and people would say to me, "You want to be the next Erin Andrews, right?"

"No," I always told them, "I want to be the first Lauren Sisler."

I brimmed with confidence concerning my future even though I had few experiences to base that on. Before the job in Parkersburg, I had never done any live television except a few small stories back in Roanoke. This new job gave me my first experience on live TV, but I was starting late in the game. My first broadcast happened the second week into the high school football season. Talk about getting thrown in the fire.

I remember it well and for the most embarrassing reasons. First, I was wearing a borrowed polo shirt from the station that said "Football Frenzy." Since they'd had to order a new shirt in my size, I was wearing an old one the station had in storage, and it was something like an XXL—just a bit bigger than what my gymnast frame needed. I mean, that shirt completely swallowed me.

Friday night in a local newsroom is absolute chaos for a sports department. My sports director, Jim Wharton, and I were scrambling to edit all the highlights. With my experience covering high school football as a photographer, I knew the ropes, but I was in a totally different role this time.

I grabbed the highlight scripts, sprinted to the studio, and sat at the anchor desk in front of the camera, totally out of breath. The little red tally light flickered on. It was showtime. I was live. I was smiling. And I was a hot mess!

The opening credits rolled by, and then Jim started talking. "Hello, and welcome to Football Frenzy. I'm Jim Wharton, and we've got a new co-host on the show. Lauren, why don't you introduce yourself?"

My heart was racing, and I felt like something was lodged in my throat. I stared at the camera. Nothing came out of my mouth. I couldn't remember my name—even though Jim had just announced it—or where I was from. I completely froze. I felt like one of those old Looney Tunes where the character's face fills up with redness like a meter.

To me, time stood still as I racked my brain for any information about myself, anything at all. In fact, seconds of complete silence were ticking by, not a good thing for television. Finally, Jim picked up on what was happening, glossed things over, and kept it going. I was crushed, though!

My first time on live TV, and I had messed it up. I had spent my whole life performing in a leotard in front of a crowd of strangers, and it was no problem. Had I lost my cool? If this was how it was going to go, I was in deep trouble. I worried about what my boss would say, but it turned out that I didn't need to stress. It was a small station, and they understood my nerves as did the sweet, always-kind viewers sitting at home watching— one of the benefits of working in a close-knit, small-town community.

Over time, I got less nervous, but my apprehension never truly dissipated. To this day, I still get butterflies. In fact, that's the big reason I started dancing around the sidelines before and during a game, mic and clipboard in hand—to tamp down my nerves. It's popularly known as the *sideline shimmy*. In many ways, it's become a form of real-time therapy for me.

The jitters and thrill that rush through my body during my sideline shimmy remind me of the nerves I felt as an athlete. When I saluted the judges in gymnastics, I got the same feeling that I do when I hear, "We're on the air in—5, 4, 3, 2, 1." And I'm LIVE!

It's hard to truly replicate what it feels like to be a competitive gymnast. First, because there's no such thing as a pickup game of gymnastics. No one goes in the backyard and just competes on the bars against a friend. Consequently, when your competitive career is over, a part of you can wither away. It's like saying goodbye to a piece of yourself.

The more I spent time on air, the more I appreciated the pre-game nerves. TV reporting was my way of reproducing that feeling of competing on a big stage. Only, as a broadcast journalist, I was competing with myself instead of against a team. Now, I just want to give my best performance every time I'm on the air. Sports reporting fits me and my competitive nature perfectly!

In Parkersburg, I kept up the performance act in my personal life as well as my professional one. When anyone asked about my parents, I stuck to the story I'd invented back at Rutgers: Mom died of respiratory failure, and Dad passed away from a sympathetic heart attack a few hours later. The words *drug addiction* still did not leave my mouth in connection with my parents' lives or deaths.

I wouldn't let anyone else use those words in my presence either. Aunt Linda would sometimes start to share her version of events (otherwise known as *the truth*), but every time she did so, I shut her down. Since those days, I've thought often about the reasons for my stubborn silence. I've decided that two things kept me from telling the truth. First, I didn't think random people needed to know our story (I was wrong about that). And second, it was just brutal for me to have to keep hearing it.

My aunt, though, tried to break me out of my cloistered silence. If we were in a public setting and someone asked about my parents, she would get the ball rolling by saying something like, "My sister and brother-in-law struggled with a lot of pain. They were taking prescription drugs, and things started to get out of hand."

Then I would jump in and change the subject. Or I'd say, "You know that's not what happened, Aunt Linda." Or even "Hey, Auntie, can we not talk about this right now?"

Later, she and I would argue about what had transpired and who needed to know. "You are attacking their legacy," I would tell her. "If you don't stop, others will think Mom and Dad were bad people."

"No one who matters will think that," Aunt Linda would reply. "The people who loved your parents will always love them, no matter what."

I didn't agree. Authenticity is not as straightforward as some may think.

Years after Mom and Dad died, I still firmly believed that their legacy was bound in my hands, and it was up to me to preserve it. I viewed anyone who would say a negative word about them or their deaths as an enemy. When my aunt would tell the truth, it seemed like she had turned into their enemy, which made the situation even more painful.

I remained rooted in my conviction not to read the toxicology reports; I still didn't want to face the truth. I could never acknowledge that Mom had put a drug in the freezer, never accept that she wanted a bigger high to take away all her pain even if only temporarily.

In my self-deception, I believed Mom only wore the patch the way the doctor prescribed it. That was the only reason for fentanyl being in her system. The patch must have leaked, I insisted. Too much medicine seeped in. That's what killed her.

When people looked at me a little funny after hearing my version of events, I attributed their reaction to ignorance. Other people just didn't understand my mom. If they knew her as I did, they'd know she overdosed accidentally. So why even mention that part? To me, the drugs were irrelevant to their deaths.

When it came to Dad's story, I felt especially sensitive. His addiction, after all, was more clearly defined than Mom's had been. I would crack a little every now and then when telling Mom's story and admit a partial truth: "My mom was in a lot of pain and might have gotten her medications mixed up by accident." But I kept a hero's silence about Dad's addiction issues. The events surrounding his death left me feeling even more raw than my mom's death, and I worked to avoid the subject entirely.

For much of my life, my father struggled with drinking too much as a way to cope with his PTSD, stemming from his military experiences. When the drinking began to affect his everyday life, including his marriage and relationship with us, he sought out medical treatment and counseling for alcoholism. He relapsed several times, however.

After each relapse, my mother would tell him that he needed to be more diligent about attending his Alcoholics Anonymous meetings. She was dismayed and fed up, but she always forgave him and loved him through his setbacks. Dad also suffered from severe esophagitis and a chronic back condition that required the surgeon to place a permanent spinal cord stimulator. My father, like my mother, experienced a lot of pain and was prescribed heavy doses of different medications.

The fentanyl patches, though, were hers, not his. The truth of the matter (that I tried desperately to ignore) was that Dad needed a bigger high because what he was prescribed just didn't satisfy him anymore, and I couldn't escape that fact. It wasn't Mom's idea to freeze the fentanyl patches and suck out the gel. That was Dad's scheme.

However, the end result was the same. Mom followed right along behind Dad, turning a medical prescription for back pain into a full-blown addiction for physical and emotional comfort. But Dad—my hero—was perhaps the one who led the way into the darkness that eventually enveloped them both.

It was a darkness I couldn't imagine, or maybe I just didn't want to think about it, so I pushed all thoughts of their addiction out of my mind. My logic felt solid: Mom and Dad weren't doing street drugs. They were only taking what the doctor prescribed for legitimate medical concerns. My parents were in a lot of pain, and those meds made them feel better. There couldn't be anything wrong with taking them ... right?

My rationalizations went round and round in my brain.

Back then, I hadn't been through recovery. I didn't understand the world of an addict. I only knew the stigmas and the stereotypes. I knew what I'd seen on TV or in the movies. I knew the old tropes about crackheads and dope dealers and drug-infested gangs. That wasn't Mom and Dad. They were respectable, educated, solidly middle-class American citizens who faithfully attended church and gave their children a lovely upbringing. Nothing about their lives matched my image of a drug addict.

Unfortunately, my image of addiction was incorrect and incomplete. I didn't know that drug addicts come from every age, race, gender, religion, and socio-economic background. Money can't protect you from substance abuse, and neither can education, patriotism, or a loving family.

In addiction prevention groups, we ask ourselves: *What is a drug addict? When we think about an addict, what images come to mind? Who told you about addiction when you were growing up?*

Someone created a vision of addiction for us, and it probably wasn't a complete picture. The truth is that for every homeless man shooting up heroin under a bridge, a classy professional is snorting coke in a bathroom with gold-plated faucets.

Since my parents didn't fit my very limited image of an addict, it was impossible for me to think that they could have been addicted to drugs. The very hint of that suggestion wrenched me at the gut level, so I took every piece of information that contradicted my story and put it on the shelf, storing them for safekeeping until I was ready to reach for those memories.

The funny thing about that behavior—the extremely private, quiet unwillingness to share with others—is that I'm not like that at all. Normally I'm an open book, ruthlessly honest in fact. In that way, I'm just like my mom. She would tell you anything. Also like my mom, we both compartmentalized the facts concerning her addiction. Mom wouldn't tell anyone what she was doing or get help for herself. I wouldn't tell anyone what she did or use her story to help others.

How could an honest person like me become such a dang good liar?

*Photographer and grip for Friday
Football Extra at WDBJ7*

DJ Sizzler on the 1s and 2s

*On the anchor desk at WTAP
(Left: Sports director Jim Wharton on Football Frenzy
Right: Lauren "Wepp" Weppler and Leslie Barrett)*

25

Seven Years of Patience

EVEN THOUGH I HAD PRACTICED LYING FOR SEVERAL YEARS, something began to shift in me while I lived in West Virginia. It's strange how time plays with your perceptions. By this point, seven years had passed since the night my parents died. Seven years of anger, hurt, healing, and then humility. I began to recognize something I had missed in the middle of my pain; I recognized all the wonderful people who had held my hands and helped me learn to walk again when I no longer needed to be carried.

When I realized the beautiful way people stuck by my side during my darkest moments, I started to bring my secrets to light. Cautiously, I began cluing people in about what really happened. Just a little. With my heart pounding, I'd talk with close friends about how Mom and Dad struggled with pain and took prescription drugs for it.

I filled in a few gaps with information derived from my storyteller's imagination—always making excuses for them. "Oh, they were in so much pain that they needed their medications to function. It was a tough struggle, but my parents pushed through it."

I said it like they were the heroes of the story, not its victims or its villains. Even with these scraps of truth, however, I never revealed the link between prescription drugs and my parents' deaths. I stuck by my stories of respiratory failure and a heart attack on the same night by two people who—in totally unrelated news—just happened to be taking a lot of prescription painkillers. I allowed a little more truth into the story, but I let it remain mostly a lie.

My deceptions were so flimsy that even I could see through them. The web of half-truths I insisted on spinning was trapping me tighter all the time, and I couldn't live in it.

Aunt Linda came to see me one weekend, and she stayed at my condo in Parkersburg. One night, I invited a colleague to come to my house and have dinner with us. Her first name was also Lauren, and her last was Weppler. She called me Sis. I called her Wepp.

Since I was still new to the Parkersburg station, Wepp didn't know me very well or have any clue about my story. She and I were just starting to get close, and I had only briefly mentioned Mom and Dad.

As I was in the kitchen getting dinner ready, Wepp and Aunt Linda were sitting on the couch in my living room. Over the sound of the TV in the background, I could hear Aunt Linda reminiscing, sharing memories about my parents. All of a sudden, she launched into the story of their addiction and death.

Snippets of their conversation drifted my way...

"...this has been tough on the family..."

"We were all so close..."

"...yeah, Lauren was especially tight with her parents..."

My heart pounded as I walked into the living room where they sat. Even when I came into the room, Aunt Linda never missed a beat of her story. She didn't cover each detail of their drug abuse and their deaths, but she did talk about chronic pain, how Mom was seeing a pain management doctor, and how both of my parents struggled to manage their pain medication.

Instead of cutting her off as I had done every time for the last seven years, I crept back into the kitchen, silent.

From my place at the stove, I could still hear what was happening in the living room. More than that, I could sense in my spirit what was going on, and I did nothing to interfere. I didn't barge into the room and change the subject; I didn't try to shut my aunt down or push her away. I didn't look daggers at her to get her to be quiet. I just listened and stayed out of the conversation.

It was the first time I ever let my aunt tell the truth about my parents' deaths, so it was the first time I heard someone react to the real story. To my surprise, Wepp responded with deep compassion and without judgment. She just said how proud my parents must be of who I was.

Emboldened by my reaction that night, Aunt Linda began to share our family's story more freely. Over time, I got to the point where I would nod in agreement. No voice. Just a brief nod here and there. Eventually, I started to interject something into the story—not a defense of my parents, simply an acknowledgment that what my aunt said was true.

Even though she spoke the truth, Aunt Linda always did so in love. She kept the story soft and shared about Mom's multiple surgeries, her pain, and the vast overprescription of drugs she received as a result. Aunt Linda talked about addiction in a new way, one that wasn't shameful or condescending, giving me a fresh perspective on pain and drug abuse. Most importantly, my aunt let me be myself and accept the story on my own timeline. I'm forever grateful to her for doing that.

Her seven years of patience were a remarkable gift.

Aunt Linda wasn't the only gift-giver in the family. The early and sudden deaths of my parents also forced me to receive two other gifts: perspective and perseverance. Life would soon give me a chance to use both.

In TV, you usually sign an agreement to stay in one location for two or three years. About six months before your contract expires, you decide if you want to stay or move on. My two-year contract at WTAP expired in 2011, and I chose to look for greener grass—really, greener football fields.

That September, I landed a job as a sports anchor and reporter with CBS 42 in Birmingham, Alabama. The station was much bigger, and it seemed like a good career move for me, so I jumped in with both feet. That season, the station put me on the road following the Alabama and Auburn football teams alongside veteran sportscaster Jim Dunaway as my guide and mentor, teaching me the ins and outs of college football coverage in the south.

While I did get to interview star athletes and stand on the fields of all the biggest college stadiums, traveling as a sports journalist turned out to be a far cry from the glamorous life some may imagine. I stayed in cheap, run-of-the-mill hotels because that's all the station had the budget for.

One morning, I sat in a hotel lobby eating my usual continental breakfast of waffles and Lucky Charms when I happened to glance at the TV, which was so tiny that it was sitting on top of the refrigerator. I had to squint a little to see the screen. College GameDay, ESPN's flagship program, was on, and Sam Ponder, a blond female sportscaster about my age, was reporting. Incredibly talented, Sam's personality and charisma shone through the miniature screen.

Seeing Sam—someone my own age who already stood at the pinnacle of our profession while I sat in a dumpy little hotel eating waffles and cereal—stung me badly. At that time, I was nowhere close to reaching her level of success, and I had been working my tail off ever since I graduated college.

The questions started rolling through my mind: *What does my career timeline look like? When was my turn coming? Would I ever be successful?*

Those questions continued to mount as I started comparing myself to all the other sports reporters and athletes who were making it big—bigger than I was. I kept playing the comparison game for several weeks. Before long, that mindset started to erode my confidence. I believed my dreams were unattainable.

I bounced back and forth between two perspectives. On one hand, I had only been at my new job for a year, and good things take time. Maybe I needed to focus on my present position instead of the future unknowns. But on the other hand...

Maybe I wasn't cut out for this job. Maybe I couldn't make it in the sports industry. Maybe all of this really was too difficult for me.

The *what-ifs* and the *maybes* began to torture me.

Ironically, these fears became the soil in which my work as a sports journalist began to grow. Early on in my career, I had been enamored with how cool it was to be on TV. All my life, I had enjoyed performing, and being in the spotlight gave me a feeling of significance. That was part of what made gymnastics so rewarding for me—getting to perform for the pleasure and applause of others. When I accomplished something particularly challenging as a gymnast, I took pride in showing other people what hard work and determination could do.

I found that being on TV offered many of the same emotional benefits, and it was something I could imagine my parents would be proud of, too. If they were still around, I just know my dad would be sitting on his recliner, remote in hand, smiling at me through the screen with my mom by his side. Before I would go live with a story, I'd look up to heaven and say, "Hey, Mom and Dad, I'm on TV." And every single time, I'd imagine them smiling back down at me. Proud. So proud of their little girl. I envisioned that scene, and their reactions, over and over and over again until my life as a broadcast journalist somehow became intertwined with my parents' deaths.

Even though my viewers at home knew nothing of my background, I treated my TV career as a chance to redeem my parents' bad choices through my own successes. If thousands of people could see me, a successful, happy, and healthy woman on TV, then they would know that I must have had solid parents who raised me and helped me get to that point. I was still protecting Mom and Dad. Still trying to hold their legacy in my hands. Still curating their stories instead of living my own.

With the clarity that only experience and hindsight can provide, I now see how sad that thinking really was.

Eventually, my skewed motivations changed as—slowly—I started to fall in love with my story. As I accepted the truth of my parents' addiction and deaths, the shame that had once held me shackled and helpless fell from me, and I also began to look at my career differently. I found new courage and strength that had nothing to do with my accomplishments or my role as a public figure. Instead, it had everything to do with my character and my mission; my purpose is to tell stories that impact others' lives in a positive way.

I chose to let my story slip out of my hands and into God's hands, and He led me back to my purpose. I discovered that no matter how much success I would attain through my career, it would never fulfill me; success and fame weren't my purpose.

To fulfill my mission, I need to be honest and forthright, qualities I had intentionally avoided for seven years. I have to find and tell the stories of men and women who inspire others to pursue their best lives. That's what I want my legacy to be; that's what I hope to be known for—changing lives through the power of story. Grasping firmly onto my calling, I realized that we are all much more than those labels we inherit. My parents weren't just addicts, and I am not just a sportscaster; I am a storyteller and difference-maker.

Every time I walk out on the field now, I have the same conversation with God. "Dear Lord, grant me the ability and the discernment to share great stories that inspire others."

As my own legacy began to take shape, I felt guilt for letting it interfere with my long-held desire to protect my parents' legacy. The question was growing clearer and more insistent: Would I devote the rest of my days to safeguarding my parents' reputations, or would I live my own story and fulfill my own purpose? The time was coming when I would have to choose.

*Reporting from the 2013 Iron Bowl in Auburn with
veteran sportscaster Jim Dunaway on CBS 42*

*Aunt Linda, one of my biggest cheerleaders, joined me on
the set of SEC Nation in Athens, Georgia, in 2017.*

26

The First Woman in the
Alabama Football Walk of Fame

HE SOLUTION TO MY DILEMMA CAME FROM AN UNEXPECTED source—Nick Saban. Alabama's head coach from 2007 to 2023, Nick is going to go down in history as one of the greatest football coaches of all time. Shortly after my first interactions with him, I left quite the impression. Literally! I left such an impression, in fact, that I almost got fired. Well, at least that's what I thought at the time.

It was A-Day of April 2012, a bit of a Roll Tide Saint's Day. I had only been in the state since the previous September, so this day was going to be my introduction to how they do football in the South, even in the spring season. And believe me, they don't just *do* football in the South. Football *is* the South.

I'll let Marino Casem, the longtime coach at Southern University, explain it. He said, "On the East Coast, football is a cultural experience. In the Midwest, it's a form of cannibalism. On the West Coast, it's a tourist attraction. And in the South, football is a religion, and Saturday is the holy day."

Yes, even though A-Day featured a scrimmage rather than an actual game, it was still a holy day. The whole event was quite a spectacle. To give you an idea of just how big of a deal it is, I'll give you the stats:

At Rutgers in New Jersey, we might have had 5,000 people in the stands for a spring game. *Maybe*. By contrast, about 50,000 fans show up for Alabama A-Day, enough to fill up half of Bryant-Denny Stadium—for a scrimmage. The stadium at Rutgers didn't even house 50,000 fans back in the early 2000s when I was there.

Thousands of foam fingers, painted faces, and zealous superfans rushed around me as if to say, "Welcome to spring football in Alabama, Lauren!"

Just a few hours before kickoff, all the pregame pageantry and festivities were in full swing, and the tailgaters had already enjoyed several burgers and beers. Along with a few thousand other people, I was standing at the University of Alabama's campus' epicenter, Denny Chimes. It's a tower right in the middle of the quad and centrally located on University Boulevard, about 300 yards from the stadium.

A walkway called the Walk of Fame runs around Denny Chimes. It's where the captains from previous years come back to the school and leave their handprints and cleat prints in wet cement, preserving their legacy for posterity. Beside the prints, their name is etched on a block, and the whole pageant is a big deal for the university, football program, and state. It's like the Alabama version of Hollywood's Walk of Fame.

That day, the other reporters and I—along with the crowds—were waiting for Coach Saban and the players to come back and memorialize the team captains. My photographer tapped me on the arm. "Hey, Lauren, can you hustle up to the stadium and grab the tripod?"

"Do we have time?" I asked him.

"Run," he said. "It's 300 yards away. You have tennis shoes on. You can make it."

"Alright, I got this," I told him.

So in true Lauren Sisler fashion, I went sprinting down the road, which had been blocked off to traffic. I got to our station's satellite truck, opened it, and grabbed the tripod. At that exact moment, I heard the sirens indicating that Saban and the players were en route to Denny Chimes. I kicked it up to jet speed, running with the tripod in hand through blocked-off areas of the campus. Back at the media holding area, I flashed my credentials for entrance and then looked around for my photographer.

I spotted him, standing on the other side of a drove of reporters who had gathered in a circle like vultures over roadkill. I darted through the middle of the crowd, already proud of myself for making it back in time. I locked eyes with my colleague, then SPLAT!

I looked down and saw that my foot was stuck in the wet cement reserved for Nick Saban and his captains. I had just enshrined myself forever in the Walk of Fame (or Shame, in my case). As soon as I sensed the soft suck of wet cement around my new white tennis shoe, I felt sick.

Maybe no one had noticed? I looked around in hope.

Everyone had noticed. Some people thought it was hysterical—mostly the other reporters. But many were furious. This accident was sacrilege to them, and they looked ready to cast stones. They had prepared everything to a tee, just like the Alabama Process, and by putting one foot wrong, I had messed it all up.

The sirens were getting closer and closer, and so was my doom. At the same time, Twitter was apparently blowing up with the story that some girl had put her foot in the wet cement at Alabama. *Way to get your 30 seconds of fame in there, Lauren*. A reporter from another station took one look at my shoe and said, "You're going to get fired."

Suddenly, there before me stood a man with a bucket in one hand, a spatula in the other, and—as far as I was concerned—a halo around his head and angel wings on his back. He said, "Yeah, we expected this to happen. We prepared for someone like you to come along."

He smoothed over the wet concrete, removing the evidence of my transgression. But still, I was the first woman to be enshrined in Alabama's football Walk of Fame, even if it was only for a few seconds. As much as I loved the poem about footprints in the sand, I didn't want to leave mine in the concrete.

You know I've always wondered if Nick Saban ever found out about "the incident" that day. Perhaps one day I will ask him. Over the years, I've gotten to know Nick pretty well. He's inspired me—along with thousands of other people—with his colorful wisdom. My favorite saying of his to this day is "Be where your feet are." Maybe we should add to the end of that, "But don't put your feet in wet concrete."

I added his quote to my mantra. Be where your feet are. Don't look behind you. The past is out of your control now. Don't look ahead. The future will give you anxiety. Put all your concentration on the present moment.

In football, as in life, it's easy to get ahead of yourself. Players start thinking about the SEC Championship instead of the game they're in. That kind of thinking is a trap, and it will lead you into serious trouble. It's so easy to assume your current opponent isn't going to be tough to beat, and you find yourself in an upside-down situation on the field.

I find myself struggling against those same thoughts. People often say to me, "Lauren, what's your 10-year plan? When are you going to move up? What are you going to do next? Do you want to be a … (and they will fill in the blank with whatever they want me to be)?"

Trying to run ahead of my feet has been my lifelong Achilles heel. When we lived in the pea-green trailer, I wanted to live in a house. When we lived in a house, I wanted to live at college. When I was at college, I wanted to be working. When I was working, I wanted a better job, a bigger city, and a glitzier career.

But you know what I found out? Time is non-refundable. Every second I had with my parents was a gift. Do you know how easy it is to take a gift for granted? To focus on the future instead of on what you have in the present?

Had I known I would only have 18 years with Mom and Dad, I would have cherished the time more. I would have lived in the moment. I wouldn't have rushed ahead of myself.

These days, I just want to be where my feet are because that's where I'm supposed to be. I'm happy with where I am. Every morning when I wake up, I take great joy and pride in my gifts and the chance to share those gifts with others. I've been given a powerful story, and now that I have accepted it, I can use my voice to tell it and be an advocate for others.

I believe my experience can be universal—recognizing the power of your story ultimately leads you back to your purpose. Like everyone else God ever put on this earth, I have a unique purpose to fulfill and a story to tell. I realized that if I wanted to tell my story in a way that mattered, I needed to change my perspective and focus on the present rather than striving for the future.

I said I inherited two gifts from my parents—perspective, and perseverance. Sticking my foot in the concrete helped me with perspective. For perseverance, I once again took hold of a Nick Saban quote. During a coaches meeting before a game, I asked him about a specific player on the team who had to sit and wait his turn. This guy really went through adversity before he got an opportunity to become a key player in a starting role.

Before answering, Coach Saban looked at me hard. Then he said, "Perseverance is synonymous with being successful."

When you see Alabama, or any other top team, playing in a game, you only witness the results of their practice. You don't see the 6:00 a.m.

workouts, the hours of film, the criticism from coaches, the grueling summer sprints. Anyone who competes at a high level must persevere to overcome adversity.

Even the most athletic person in the world will not succeed in sports without perseverance. That truth was driven home in me earlier in my career when I was a reporter for a program that aired on Saturdays. I had various assignments for each show, some pre-recorded and some live.

As I was waiting for my next live hit, I quietly watched our show on the big screen TV next to the set. During one of the segments, an incredibly inspiring feature story ran on a player who lost his dad tragically. The whole saga hit close to home, and I knew in the depths of my soul what that player was experiencing. I also knew I shouldn't engage with it emotionally, but I did. I lost it.

I couldn't stop sobbing, but I had to compose myself because my segment was coming up after the next commercial break. I found some tissues and put my game face back on. As I wiped away the tears streaming down my face, I looked over and saw someone crack a smile. They nudged the person beside them, pointed at me, and laughed out loud. It made me feel a bit shamed for openly displaying my emotions; I felt like I needed to apologize. But for what?

That was a turning point in my life because I realized in an instant that we all experience life differently.

Those who haven't experienced deep trauma simply cannot relate on a personal level with those who are going through a crisis. People who haven't had to persevere through life's deepest hell may not have empathy for those who have. Of course, I wish I could bring my parents back, but I also see what happened to us as a gift because I can use it in a positive way. I pray that my own trauma gives me a chance to understand others and contribute to their success.

My success as a sports reporter might look different than your success as a mom, a lawyer, a construction manager, or whatever your role is. We can, however, all help each other persevere along the way.

In late December of 2011, Alabama went to the national championship in my first football season in Birmingham. If you're a sports reporter, you work all of football season, and at the end of it, management decides if you're going to take one for the team, stay home, and anchor from the studio, or if you're going to the national championship. I was sure I had put in the long hours, the late nights, and the hard work needed to go to the championship in New Orleans.

The cards weren't in my favor, however, and they picked me to stay behind. I was, shall we say, not thrilled. Okay, I'll admit it: I was deeply disappointed. I had put in just as much hard work as everyone else, but still, I was the one who had to sit at home while the others stood on the sideline of the most exciting college football game of the year.

Even through my disappointment, I did have one good thing to look forward to that week; Uncle Mike and Aunt Linda were coming to visit me in Birmingham. They were on their way to the Sugar Bowl to watch Virginia Tech play Michigan, and when they stopped in to see me, I took them to a restaurant called Tavern at the Summit, one of my favorite spots in the metro area.

Our waiter, we'll call him Tom, chatted with us as he took our orders. He even recognized me from the local CBS news station. "Shouldn't you be in New Orleans?" he asked.

I explained the situation, and we talked briefly about Alabama football. At the end of dinner, I excused myself to visit the bathroom. Aunt Linda and Uncle Mike, who have never met a stranger in their lives, took up chatting with the waiter in my absence.

It was three years before I found out what transpired that night while I was away from the table.

As usual, Aunt Linda had taken the conversation with our waiter to a deeper level than appetizers and aperitifs. "Lauren's got an interesting story," she told Tom. "You should Google her."

According to my auntie, that was all she said. The waiter thanked her for the suggestion. When I came back to the table, we paid the bill and left. The evening most slipped from my mind.

Our waiter, however, went home and did exactly what Aunt Linda had told him to do. He Googled me. By this time, I had recorded a few clips for YouTube and other sites talking a little about what happened to my mom and dad.

Long into the night, Tom sat in his room, listening to the clips I'd recorded, crying while he heard my story unfold. As it turns out, our waiter was an addict himself. Growing up in a well-to-do, picture-perfect family, addiction wasn't supposed to be in the cards for Tom—just like it wasn't supposed to happen to my parents. And just like them, it was prescription pain pills that snagged Tom.

As a teenager, Tom worked for a moving company as his summer job. While working, Tom and his buddies would scout out the wealthy homes where they knew the owners likely had the money—and the desire—for the prescriptions the boys were interested in. Once they'd found their target and been hired for the moving job, Tom would raid the pill cabinets and swipe some of the medicine for himself.

Although he had been clean for years before he met me, Tom had never opened up about his story. He was afraid of judgment, what people would think. He was a good guy, not a stereotypical drug addict.

As Tom heard me tell my parents' story, he realized that he could raise the courage to tell his own story to someone besides his wife. He started with his next-door neighbor. After sharing with him, Tom discovered what it felt like to quit running and hiding from your story and to share it freely with others.

Over the next three years, Tom opened up to more and more people about his past, his hangups, and his addictions. He started volunteering with the Addiction Prevention Coalition around the same time that I became more public about my involvement with advocacy work. The whole time, I had no idea who he was, what he was doing, or that he had ever heard my story, but my honesty had started a chain reaction of healing through Tom.

After years of my descent through denial, God was preparing me for my ascent to acceptance. As my heart healed, God opened my eyes to the truth and revealed to me that my parents were defined not by how they died but by how they lived.

The truth has set me free, and now my story of great loss and tragedy has become a gift of hope and restoration for others who believe they can't be delivered from life's difficult circumstances. I know that God doesn't always deliver us *out* of hardships, but instead, he delivers us *through* hardships.

Like the "Footprints" poem says, "It was then that I carried you." I see now that he was carrying me all along, helping me to build my strength so that one day I could stand on my own two feet and begin walking forward again, offering a guiding hand to those around me who might be stumbling.

*The shoe that famously
inducted me into the
Alabama Football Walk of Fame*

*Interviewing Alabama head coach
Nick Saban after a game in 2019*

27

Nothing but the Whole Truth

IN MARCH 2013, I WALKED RIGHT INTO MY FIRST OPPORTUNITY TO share my story on television. One of our station's assistant news directors, Scott MacDowell, and reporter Kaitlin McCulley had heard about my parents. Scott happened to be doing a project with Alabama's drug task force right then, and he had some other opportunities lining up, too. He thought my story might help.

Did I want to be part of things? Well … did I? I had just started sharing my story by myself without Aunt Linda there to lean on. I was still unsure if it was okay to talk about my parents and how they died. As a woman in a male-dominated field, I had worked incredibly hard to build a career in sports journalism. What if going into addiction advocacy work meant the end of that career?

My contract at the station was about to end anyway. Was this my moment? Should I transition out of TV and into advocacy work?

I considered my options. I might have come across as the classic Southern Christian girl, but I did know all about this kind of drug addiction, and advocacy would be worthwhile work. The need for awareness and education was only growing.

News stories about drugs were pouring into the station almost daily. Drug busts were no longer about local cops arresting two-bit criminals passing dime bags on the wrong side of the street. Now, reporters were covering FBI stings against respected doctors who were running pill mills. Across America, physicians and dentists were performing medically unnecessary procedures, billing Medicaid, and then prescribing hydrocodone or other narcotics to patients they knew would abuse or sell their medication.

Almost overnight, the face of drugs in America had transformed. Modern drug kingpins weren't the South American strongmen of the '80s and '90s. They were your family doctor or dentist. And drug addicts no longer looked like the "troubled youth" of the Reagan era. Now, they looked a lot like … well, a lot like my parents.

If you had called a Hollywood casting agency and asked them to send you a drug addict look alike, they wouldn't have sent you my mom. And if you had requested a male character actor who could convince an audience that he stole his wife's prescription medication, they wouldn't have sent you my dad.

Maybe if you had asked for an all-around all-American family, though, you might have gotten us. Athletic performers. Solid students. Fun-loving friends. Good Christian people.

But across the country, people just like Mom and Dad were falling victim to the opioid epidemic. Family members like me and Allen didn't know what to say, what to look for, or how to help.

How does an all-American success story become a nightmare literally overnight? Why do people who have everything they could ever want sacrifice it all for another pill? Why do we only trust the people who tell us what we want to hear? Why don't we tell the truth instead of living a lie?

Thousands of families like mine were asking these exact questions. I didn't have all the answers for them, but I did have a story I could tell them. Maybe now I could do something about the devastation of addiction. Maybe now I *should* do something about it. I could even use my investigative journalism skills to dig into the foundation of where this stuff was coming from. Maybe this work would even give me insight into what happened to my parents.

Ten years had passed since the night Mom and Dad both died from drug overdoses, and I still didn't know where they got the prescriptions or how they got their hands on so much medication. I hadn't looked at the toxicology reports or read the medical records. I hadn't created a timeline of my parents' last minutes or even their final few months.

I didn't know that after I called Allen with the news of Mom's death, he relentlessly rang the house over and over and over again, fingers crossed that Dad would pick up. I didn't know Allen never got an answer beyond Mom's recorded voice inviting him to leave a message.

I still didn't know that a single doctor in Roanoke had prescribed hundreds of narcotics for my parents less than one month after my dad almost died of an overdose. I didn't know that this doctor was well aware of my mom's inability to control her meds, but still, he gave her greater and greater doses every time she went for an appointment. I didn't know that Aunt Linda wondered why Mom had seemed so eager to visit her pain management physician.

It was time I learned the truth.

One night, I called Aunt Linda with a request. "Will you send me the toxicology reports and the medical records about my parents?"

She was more than willing to let me have them. As soon as the reports arrived, I ripped open the envelope. I was terrified of what I would find there, but I was more afraid of going one more day without knowing the truth.

In the reports, I saw the diagrams of Mom and Dad's bodies. (Thankfully, there weren't any pictures.) Arrows pointed out the contusions and bruises. I read the key facts about what happened that night.

Until then, I didn't know Dad had collapsed or that they found blood on his face. I didn't know he had found my mom on the porch or dragged her body down the hall to the bathroom in a vain attempt to resuscitate her. I had made a lot of assumptions about their fate—all of them wrong. I had fed myself a steady diet of misinformation.

The first big lie an addict tells is to themselves. The lies we tell ourselves feel good when we're telling them, but they never do anything but harm over the long term. Some of us can be so dang good at lying to ourselves, though. And while I was an honest, by-the-book person with other people, I was also really good at lying to myself.

My mom, too, was honest and by the book when it came to managing things. That's why, when the drugs first got out of control, she thought she could manage them. But she was wrong about that, terribly, terribly wrong. The number of pills recorded on the pages in front of me proved just how deadly her miscalculation of her own strength had been.

I cried as the reports unveiled all the details of that awful night. I could only imagine Dad's sadness and distress as he sat alone in the house with Mom's body. I could only grieve over what he must have felt at finally having to call 911 and watch them try in vain for hours to bring her back.

But you know what? For as much pain as I found in that report, I also discovered tremendous relief by having all the facts. For years, the empty holes in the story had created such darkness in my mind. The gaps in the timeline had brought me so much uncertainty. Now, I had a new sense of peace; I didn't need to lie anymore to others or myself.

Back when my parents died, I had wanted to know *why it happened*. Why our family? Why my parents? Once I learned more about addiction and began to understand some of these reasons, my concerns turned to *how it happened*. The medical reports answered many of these questions with facts that, instead of scaring me, actually soothed my feelings.

Don't get me wrong; knowing how my parents died doesn't change what happened. No amount of information can ever undo death. But knowing the facts removed the burden of needing to fix their story; it was never my job to fix everything—or even to fix anything.

Knowing the facts doesn't reverse life's tragedies, but it does make it possible to tell your story more effectively. Once I understood what happened, I was better positioned to be an advocate for people who feel like they've been silenced by shame. Having some answers allowed me to speak on behalf of my parents, even to honor them. After all, they had been silenced by their shame, and I knew they wouldn't want me to live my life with that same burden.

As soon as I finished reading the toxicology reports, I knew I was going on camera with this story. I did the video feature with Scott and Kaitlin and shared the complete story for the first time ever.

And I got the response that I never thought I'd get in a million years. People loved me, and family and friends still loved my parents just the same—just the way Aunt Linda had always assured me they would. Some people said it gave them peace, knowing the truth.

For ten long years, I had believed the lie that I had to be ashamed of what my parents did and how they died. I finally put away the facade that covered my pain, trading it for true joy. Slowly, I was learning that I could turn my family's heartache into something life-changing for other people— just as I know Mom and Dad would want me to do.

Their Little Lady Lauren was growing shameless!

28

It Started with You, Lauren

I FIRST MET TIMOTHY ALEXANDER AT A BASEBALL GAME WHERE HE was selling tickets at the front gate. It was the spring of 2012, and as the local sports reporter, I had a media credential. Timothy was a young, African-American man with a million-dollar smile and a wheelchair.

"Hey, you're the news lady, right?" he asked me.

I admitted that I was.

"I'm a big fan of yours," he said. "Can we take a picture?"

I agreed. Someone snapped our picture, and I thought no more about the interaction.

A year later, I was at Legion Field in Birmingham, watching the UAB football team practice and shooting highlights of their drills.

"Hey, Lauren!" someone yelled.

I turned around. A young man in a wheelchair was heading my direction. He was wearing his UAB jersey, and I recognized him right away.

"Timothy! How's everything going?"

"Great!" he said. "I'm on the football team now."

I looked at his wheelchair, then at his face. He radiated inspiration.

"The first time I met you," I said, "you were handing out tickets at a ticket booth, and now you're on the football team. How did this happen?"

Timothy started talking, and right away, I knew I had a story, the kind of story I had always wanted, a story that would inspire people. We exchanged phone numbers, and I set up things with the TV station. That summer, I followed Timothy everywhere. I went to practice with him. I went to rehab with him. I went to the locker room with him. I saw that everywhere he went, Timothy took a scripture verse, a motivational quote, or just a word for the day. Every word that came out of his mouth was profound.

Finally, he and I both felt ready for the interview. I brought the cameras, and Timothy shared his story.

Timothy Alexander was a gifted athlete, obsessed with football. By the time he was nearing the end of his high school career at Erwin High School, he was one of the top tight ends in the state of Alabama.

Timothy had passion on his own, but his brother, David Woodard, spurred him on even further, encouraging him on the field and even saving Timothy's life. On April 1, 2006, Timothy's house caught on fire, and his brother got him out.

Just two weeks later, tragedy struck again, however, when David was involved in a car accident that took his life.

Timothy recalled a time before a high school football game when his brother shared some words of encouragement. "'Tim, I want you to be the best you can be. If you want to go to the NFL, I want you to aim high and go. I want you to always remember that I love you.' When he told me that, and the next day he died in this car wreck and had to go through that, I told myself that I would leave everything out on the field for him."

Timothy pursued his football career with passion, and he had big plans for his future. Those plans changed, though, on October 28, 2006, when Timothy himself was involved in a serious car accident on his way to the Magic City Classic with two friends and a friend's young child.

After his friend fell asleep behind the wheel on the highway, the car smashed into an overpass guardrail. Timothy realized that he was badly injured, and the car then started to roll off a cliff. He was unable to open any doors, but he managed to use his football strength to punch a hole in the window just in time to toss the toddler out of the car before it fell to the bottom of the cliff. The event paralyzed Timothy from the neck down, and doctors said that he would never walk again.

"It happened so quickly," Timothy said. "One day I was walking, and the next day I was rolling."

But that didn't stop Timothy from pursuing his dreams. His determination and heart landed him a spot on the football roster at UAB. Timothy Alexander, number 87.

"I thank God for Coach Garrick McGee," said Timothy. "I told him, 'I am going to be one of the greatest football players that ever came through UAB. God told me that.' Coach McGee looked at me and said, 'I want you a part of this program because it took heart,' and this is what sparked the moment. He always talked about what started the blaze."

In our interview, Timothy also talked about the impact the rest of his family and friends have had on his life including his mother, grandfather, and pastor. "As long as I believe, and we all believe as one, then all things are possible," said Timothy. "If you have that winning mentality in every aspect of life you will always win."

"Timothy is a winner because he has never given up," I said as I recorded my closing standup. "Now he sets out to share that winning mentality with the rest of the world."

Later that week, I met Timothy and his mom, Patricia, at a UAB pep rally to gather a little more video for my feature. Timothy and his mom were ecstatic about the story, just like me. He sent me a text that afternoon. "Lauren, we're family now. I love you, sis!"

I cried when I read it.

Timothy's story aired on our local station in August. Later that season, a national network saw it on the news server. They came to Alabama and did a story on him as well. We didn't let our smiles drop for weeks.

Then, more tragedy happened.

UAB shut down its football program, the first NCAA Division I Football Bowl Subdivision to shutter a program in 20 years. I was there the day President Ray Watts told the players to pack their bags and go home. Football was over.

Full-grown collegiate athletes were sobbing. Football had been their life. As an athlete myself, I understood just what these kids were losing. When your team is no more, you lose your family, your focus, and everything you've worked for.

Suddenly, Timothy Alexander, the football player who let no adversity slow him down, raised his arm. "We're gonna fight this thing, and we're gonna get through this."

Right then, he became the face of the return of UAB football. At every rally, he was there. At every event, he showed up. On every publication, he was front and center.

And on Sept. 2, 2017, UAB kicked off in front of 45,212 fans. Guess who was on the field? Timothy Alexander. Except this time, he wasn't in a wheelchair. He walked on the field, stood in the lights, and held up the ball. Timothy can only walk short distances and then only with a lot of support, but with each step he takes, he defies the odds. At his wedding the following May, Timothy even walked partway down the aisle to meet his bride,

Kayla. Sitting among the congregation, I was a teary-eyed mess just watching him.

Today, Timothy is speaking all over the country, showing up at leading companies like Nike and Netflix as a motivational speaker. Every time I talk to him, he tells me the same thing. "It started with you, Lauren."

It didn't really start with me. I just helped him tell his story. But when I did, something shifted in Timothy's mindset. He saw the power one person's story could have on other people. And when I saw the power of Timothy Alexander's story, my mindset shifted too. I went from being just a sports reporter to a woman living out my calling as a storyteller with a purpose.

My first interview with Timothy Alexander   *At the UAB Football pep rally with Timothy Alexander*

29

Falling in Love with My Story

NOW THAT MY PARENTS' ADDICTIONS WERE OUT IN THE OPEN, new opportunities to serve in the addiction prevention community started rolling in.

Mentoring at the Foundry, a faith-based recovery center in Bessemer, Alabama, came into my life after meeting Randy and Beverly McClendon. Their daughter, Kimberly, had overcome her addiction through a recovery center in Mississippi. Her parents had no prior understanding of addiction and were shocked to learn about their daughter's struggles, but at her request, they helped her get into an effective treatment program. Kimberly had been clean and sober for almost four years when she lost her life in a tragic car accident in 2004.

Although Kimberly's accident had nothing to do with drugs or alcohol, her experience inspired the McClendons to start outreach programs to help people find recovery and to support families who have lost loved ones to addiction. They made a generous donation to The Foundry, and the hallways of the building's fourth floor were lined with beautiful artwork centered around one primary theme—angels.

Those angels are representative of their sweet daughter and the light she continues to shine on this world, even in her physical absence. She is an angel indeed, just like her mother and father, whom I now refer to as my "Birmingham parents." They have taken me under their wing as if I were one of their own. I firmly believe our meeting was divine, and it has opened more doors than I ever imagined from the moment I stepped foot in Alabama.

Through the McClendons, I started mentoring The Foundry women. I was matched with a beautiful young lady in her mid-20s, Audrey, and I got to work with her during certain phases of the one-year recovery program.

I watched her graduate from the program, and now I get to cheer her on as she uses her story and testimony to help others who have walked a similar path.

To celebrate Audrey's graduation, I went to Nordstrom Rack and found a beautiful cross bracelet with rhinestones. The woman who checked me out was interested in the story behind the bracelet, so I told her about my work as a mentor. She then connected me with a friend of hers, Danny Molloy, who was transitioning into a new role at an Alabama-based non-profit organization, the Addiction Prevention Coalition (APC).

In recovery himself, Danny was inspired by my story and was adamant that it needed to be heard. He invited me to volunteer at the APC, and the organization's vision soon became my mission—to help prevent substance abuse and relapse by inspiring and educating people to live with hope, resilience, and purpose.

It's amazing how one conversation can lead to life-changing experiences. There was a domino effect of honesty and hope, and all of it started with my decision to share my story and proudly brag about my mentee's successes. And now, I'm contributing to the recovery world, becoming an advocate, and helping other people through their addiction struggles.

And the opportunities just kept coming. One day, while I was at the APC, Danny approached me. "Lauren, you're a sports reporter. Would you help us make some videos to use on social media?"

What could I say? Of course, I would! Telling my story along with people whose stories were so much like mine gave me a deep sense of purpose. I knew that I was doing the right thing by opening up about my parents' lives, addictions, and deaths. But I also shared the hope that I had found in God, my family, my community, and myself.

That year while serving as a board member at the APC, I met Mat and Kathy Whatley. Acquaintances for just a time, our relationship has since grown to be profound and life-changing. Mat and Kathy have provided funding and support for various advocacy projects that I've launched, including the documentary I produced, *Beyond the Shadows*, a major undertaking and yet another step on my newfound mission.

While I continued to make connections, most of the opportunities to share my story were on a smaller scale. I spoke freely to athletic groups, community clubs, and circles of people in recovery. I felt confident that I was on the right path, but God wasn't content to let my story stay in the shadows. Through his sovereign grace, in 2016, I walked onto a larger stage and opened up about my life. Over the next three years, I told my story more times than I could count to far more people than I could have imagined.

One day shortly after Timothy Alexander heard me speak, he told me I needed a tagline because "you're a professional speaker now, Lauren." The perfect line came to me almost instantly—Fall in love with your story.

That's my message in a single phrase. I tell people my story and how I unlocked the shackles of shame. I talk about the value of sharing your story with others and the freedom that comes with learning to fall in love with it.

I believe that the stories we tell others become our reality.

I had grown a lot in the 10 years since I threw the toxicology reports on the floor of my aunt's car, hadn't I? Why did it take me so long? Why couldn't I have accepted the truth sooner?

Often, people ask me if I regret that silent decade of my life, and yes, I used to beat myself up about it. For a while, I thought I could have helped more people—had a more profound impact on the world—if I had started down this track right after I graduated from Rutgers.

Why did I keep myself shackled to shame for so long? Because you don't fall in love overnight. Oh, you might think you have. But you can't learn to love your story on page one any more than you can force yourself to fall in love on date one. Love doesn't happen in a flash. Not deep love. Genuine love opens up gently. It comes with time, patience, and commitment. You get there step by step.

As I look back over my story, I can see how every step I took—and those where God carried me—got me to where I am now. Life really is a set of footprints in the sand, not a pole vault across the beach. Every single step I've taken has been instrumental in the next one. If I had leaped into this work back in the early days, I don't think my mind, ears, eyes, or heart would have been open to receiving the opportunities I've been given.

Part of the journey through grief is the healing you experience along the way. You can't skip processing your trauma, can't fast-forward to the good part. My competitive spirit doesn't like that. I don't want to train. I want to compete. I want to win!

Let me tell you, though, that coping with grief is the skill that has taken me the longest to get into the win column. But that's okay. Overnight victories rarely last long—not in life, not in football, and not in healing. Victory takes time.

As I've opened up about my story, I've realized the significance of other people's stories—the athletes, coaches, fans, and communities I get to appreciate and interview. As a sports reporter, I have covered some of the most prolific coaches and athletes ever to coach and play the game. Ingrained in my mind is an amazing vision of confetti falling on the field after a championship.

That confetti to me isn't just a championship. It's not about the wins and losses. That confetti represents a story, layers of stories in fact. And like those athletes and coaches, we all have a story, and each story has its shameful parts. I have never met a person who didn't feel a stigma, whether it was from addiction or something else.

No single story exists on its own. We are all characters in a larger story, and the whole, big story God is telling with our lives only makes sense when we all speak up about our parts in it.

At a fundraiser for The Foundry with my "Birmingham parents,"
Randy and Beverly McClendon (and my husband, John)

Falling in love with my story on stage at a
speaking event at Radford University in 2021
(Photo by Ashlea Hough/Radford University)

30

Finding My Sideline Shimmy and Winning an Emmy

IN 2016, ALLEN SOLD THE FAMILY HOUSE IN VIRGINIA TO JOHN AND Randa Freeborn, a family living up the mountain from us. Like my parents, John and Randa thought of the house as their dream home. They moved in, fixed it up, and landscaped the yard beautifully—just the way Mom and Dad had always dreamed of doing.

Randa kept Mom's irises as part of the new landscape. She sends me photos every spring when the flowers are in bloom. Dad's birthday is the first day of spring, and the flowers give me hope that beautiful things can burst out of dry ground after a long winter. I showed the photos to a friend.

"You do know irises transplant easily, right?" she asked me.

I hadn't known that! Randa graciously gave me eight bulbs to transplant to Alabama. They're in my front yard now. When I see them in bloom, joy and excitement spring from my heart. It's a story of rebirth, right? Of beauty for ashes, as the Bible says. I plan to take these flowers with me to any future home I may live in.

The night Allen sold the house, I had a vivid dream. In it, he and I were standing outside on the porch, the same spot where Dad found Mom dead on that night so long ago. Allen and I were peering in the window like we were characters in *A Christmas Carol*. We spotted the Freeborn family—mom, dad, son, and daughter—eating dinner and laughing together. They looked so happy. When I woke up, I knew Allen had done the right thing by closing that chapter and helping another family own their dream home.

Allen and Scout, his German Shepherd, rolled into Birmingham on my birthday that year so we could see each other more often. His presence in my life is an even better gift than the trampoline I received so long ago.

In other ways, too, 2016 led to new opportunities. I became a digital sports reporter and host for AL.com in June. Then, in October, I seized the biggest prize of my career. I became a sideline reporter for ESPN.

Not only did I get to cover college football, but I also served as a reporter and analyst for college gymnastics. Talk about a dream come true! My mom had predicted I would be on ESPN one day, and there I was, a former gymnast, covering gymnastics. Eventually, football edged out collegiate gymnastics, and that's what I'm known for now.

The term "sideline shimmy" has become my on-air trademark. Honestly, people recognize me sometimes and say, "Hey, you're Lauren Sisler. I've seen you on TV. You're that reporter who dances on the sidelines."

Yes, I am!

Usually, they go on to talk about my infectious energy and how I love life, and I do love life now, as evidenced by my sideline shimmy. When I dance on the sideline, it's because I'm slightly scared of what comes next, but I'm choosing to celebrate instead of living in fear.

My relationship with Nick Saban blossomed after I stamped my foot in his walk of fame. In fact, Nick was how I won an Emmy. The story didn't start with him, though.

It actually started with Charles Barkley whom I met at the Iron Bowl. He asked me if my parents named me after the Sizzler (Sisler) steakhouse. His comment launched a great friendship between us.

One night, I was having dinner with Charles and a bunch of his friends. He brought up Nick Saban. "As an Auburn guy," Barkley said, "I have to admit it. Nick Saban is going to go down as one of the greatest coaches of all time."

As a journalist, I couldn't let that statement go without a question. "Charles, have you ever met Nick Saban? Ever talked to him?"

"Only in passing," he told me. "But I'd love to meet with him someday."

"What if I set up an interview?" I asked.

"As long as I don't have to pull any strings."

I got right to work and pitched the idea to Alabama football's sports information director. The response came quickly. Nick was interested, a rare occurrence.

In August 2016, I was working for AL.com, Alabama's state news site, when they asked me to produce a feature with Nick Saban and Charles Barkley. I could not have been handed two bigger names in sports—or two men with more contrasting personalities.

On one side, I had Charles Barkley, an international superstar, basketball player, and sports commentator. He's witty and genuine, an Auburn guy through and through. What you see is what you get. On the other side, I had Nick Saban, structured and process-oriented, and of course, he's Alabama to the core. Nick never flies by the seat of his pants.

I was charged with bringing together these two sports giants for what was supposed to be a legendary conversation. It was an amazing opportunity, not only for my career but also for me as a person. These men had so much wisdom to share.

The interview turned out to be a smashing success, winning the 2017 Southeast Regional Emmy Award for Outstanding Sports Interview. In the course of their conversation, these two sports legends talked about giving players second chances. When a player makes a mistake, Charles said, you don't kick them off the team. You create opportunities for them to learn from their mistakes, and you use those teaching moments to help them make better choices.

As he was talking, I realized that was what I wanted to do with my story. I wanted to tell families and individuals and whole communities that we all make mistakes. In the world of addiction, people make lots of mistakes, most of them willingly. It's tempting to write those folks off, dust our hands, and say, "That's it. They're hopeless. Throw them behind bars." But I think that's the exact opposite of what we should be doing. Of course, tough love is sometimes necessary, but as Nick and Charles discussed that day, we are all worthy of second chances. Maybe even third or fourth chances. If we can't extend people an opportunity to start again, then where is our hope?

Athletes mess up. Kids mess up. Addicts mess up. We all mess up; it's part of being human. We don't, however, have to define ourselves or other people by our mistakes. We get to try again.

Hope doesn't get any better than that, and I was growing more and more willing to share my story of hope with the world. Good thing, too.

Right after my parents passed, I hyper-focused on what I didn't have. Today, each time I bust a move on the football field, it's a sign that I am choosing to love life and relish my blessings even through adversity. As time has passed, it's become easier to look for the good things—the blessings that come in life.

And boy was I about to get a blessing. A double whammy of a blessing.

My mom's birthday is December 19, and when it arrived, I was already back in Roanoke, visiting family for Christmas. My friends and I decided to go to Corned Beef & Co., our old hangout where I used to deejay—you know, DJ Sizzler on the 1s and 2s. We figured we'd dance and have fun. Although it was my mom's birthday, it turned out she was the one giving a gift to me—or at least, that's how I like to think of it.

I never drink. Dance, yes. But drink, never. So there I was at the bar, Sober Sisler, ready to hit the dance floor when a guy came up and started flirting. His eyes were so bloodshot he looked like a zombie. I figured he'd been way overserved, and I wasn't interested in entertaining some drunk stranger. I found out later that, in fact, he'd just come from Lasik surgery. Just goes to show, you can't judge a book by its cover—or a guy by his eyes.

Anyway, he told me his name was John Willard. John looked way too young for me, so I asked, "How old are you?"

"23," he said.

A kid, I thought. As a mature 31-year-old, I politely turned around and continued moving about the dance floor.

My friend Trista noticed his interest, however, and encouraged him. "That girl you were just talking to?" she told him. "She's on TV. You should Google her."

Impressed by her comments, John did, in fact, Google me. As a skilled golfer, it turns out that he loves sports, too. John got my contact information and stayed in touch throughout 2016, adding even more excitement to an already big year. I had to admit that, for a 23-year-old, he was pretty amazing.

The next spring, we started long-distance dating, but that didn't last for long. After about nine months of torching the phone lines between Virginia and Birmingham, John announced he was quitting his job and moving near me.

"What will you do?" I asked him.

"I'll figure it out," he said.

And he did. John landed a great sales job in the area, eventually starting his own business, and our relationship flourished. It wasn't long before I knew he was the one. We began planning a wedding—the same wedding I'd told Aunt Linda I'd never have because no one would marry a girl without parents.

Allen and I recreated fun family memories at the racetrack at Talladega Superspeedway when he moved to Alabama.

*The conversation with Charles Barkley and
Nick Saban that won me an Emmy.*

(Photo by Ginnard Archibald/AL.com)

On the set of the SEC Network's college football pregame show SEC Nation *in 2017. I have so many fun memories reporting from college campuses around the southeast alongside (left to right) host Laura Rutledge and analysts Tim Tebow, Marcus Spears, and Paul Finebaum.*
(Photo by Scott Clarke/ESPN Images)

I found my sideline shimmy!

31

Double or Nothing

WEDDING PLANNING BROUGHT UP A LOT OF OLD HURTS AND heavy feelings. How can you plan for the best day of your life when you're constantly faced with loss?

I started seeing a therapist, Neely Haynes. As it turned out, the timing couldn't have been better since a global pandemic was about to send us all into a crisis. Here I was, planning for the happiest day of my life and feeling so, so sad at the same time. One minute I'd be strong, ready to conquer the world. The next, I'd be sitting on my bed, crying. What, I asked Neely, was wrong with me?

"Nothing's wrong. You're both happy and sad," she told me. "Happiness can't last forever. Sadness is going to creep in. But sadness doesn't last forever either. Eventually, you find healing."

Neely gave me permission to feel everything that had happened to me, the good and the bad. She was okay with me feeling the things I should feel and things I believed I shouldn't. Neely said I could be happy about marrying John and sad about losing my parents all at the same time. Instead of worrying about what I ought to feel or what someone else felt, I could just breathe.

Kids who get early training in sports learn to compartmentalize quickly. Basketball players, for example, hear the sound of the crowd just before tipoff. As soon as the ball is in the air, it gets quiet inside their heads. They've learned to focus on the challenge in front of them, not the noise around them. At that moment, they're just themselves.

It was time to transfer that athletic skill into my personal life. "Be where your feet are," Nick Saban had told me.

"Find your feet, Lauren," my therapist said.

"When you see only one set of footprints," my favorite poem told me, "it was then that I carried you."

So take a deep breath. Find your feet. Live this moment. You won't get another chance.

Well, you usually don't get another chance. I was about to get mine.

When I was a little girl, I knew exactly what my wedding day would look like. Hundreds of people would crowd into the sanctuary of our church—which in real life seated about 25 souls at best. My wedding gown would be dazzling. Dad would walk me down the aisle like a princess. Mom would be so proud, her dream of me being a wife and mother finally coming true.

My parents' deaths destroyed that childhood vision, and I was sad they wouldn't get to celebrate the big day with me. But I had discovered by now that I could either choose to focus on the people who were there or I could obsess about the people who weren't. I decided to be where my feet were.

Six-year-old me might have had my wedding designed to the last detail, but 35-year-old me had zero plans. Soon, Aunt Linda stepped in and helped me get things rolling. It would be a wedding like … well, a lot like the one that six-year-old Lauren dreamed of except with fewer frills on the dress. We would be married at Mountain Lake, a local wedding venue in Virginia, and the photos by the lake and in front of the barn would be stunning.

We scheduled our ceremony for May 30, 2020, and Aunt Linda and I stamped over 200 invitations to go in the mail. On March 11, just 11 weeks before our wedding day, the World Health Organization declared COVID-19 a pandemic, and the world shut down. I crossed my fingers and prayed hard that our two-week quarantine really would slow the spread and I could have my dream wedding.

By April 1, however, I knew it wouldn't happen. We had to cancel everything. I threw all my beautifully stamped invitations in a storage bin that was intended for all my wedding mementos, and I cried for two days. Then, I dried my eyes and rolled up my sleeves. Over my adult life, I've learned that many things don't go according to my plans, but I have to accept that with grace. I have to be nimble, make adjustments, and stick the landing as best as possible. Once again, I discovered that God had unexpected plans—this time, for my wedding day.

Yes, I said *my* wedding day.

"We'll have to put everything off," I told John in a quavering voice.

"I am marrying you on May 30, 2020," John told me.

"We can't," I said, now sobbing. "Everyone will be so afraid of the virus and the travel that they won't have fun. I want my wedding to be a joyous day."

"And I want you to be my wife," John replied. "I don't care if we go to the courthouse and say our vows. We're getting married this year."

He was right. COVID-19 might deny me the big celebration, but no way was I backing out of this marriage. We trimmed our guest list from 250 people to eight of our nearest and dearest. The big ceremony—and the march down the aisle in my dress for everyone to exclaim over—would have to wait.

We did away with nearly all the plans for wedding decor, but a kind florist in Tuscaloosa learned about my wedding being canceled and wanted to do something nice for me, so she created a gorgeous bouquet. At my suggestion, she tied the flowers together with a strip of lace from my mom's wedding dress.

Despite John's romantic suggestion of a courthouse wedding, I knew I couldn't get married any place other than the chapel at the Church of the Highlands, my faith community in Birmingham.

Other than the tiny church I'd attended with my parents back in Virginia, I'd never had a congregation become my home and family like this one had. Once I moved to Birmingham and joined the Church of the Highlands, I really began to grow in my faith. It was the place I had most often felt the love of God, and I knew it was the place I needed to be when I vowed to love John for the rest of my life. Being married in that church—instead of at the lake—by our dear friend Pastor Layne Schranz felt right. Once again, I sensed God's arms, carrying me when I didn't know what to do.

When the big day rolled around, I sat in my living room, getting my hair and makeup done. Then came a knock on the door. It was the sweet florist delivering my beautiful bouquet. She had attached a charm with my parents' wedding picture to the lace that was wrapped around the flowers. I shed my first tears of the day, but I wasn't sad at all. Not this time. I was just filled with a warmth and radiance I'd never known.

I had worried that I would focus on the empty space where Mom and Dad should have been, but from that moment on, I didn't feel my parents' absence. When the doors flung open and I stepped into the chapel, all I saw was John. Even when I walked down the aisle alone, without Dad beside me, I felt God's presence with me—as close as a father.

I love a good party, and I would never have planned a wedding with eight people, but it turned out to be just the wedding I needed. And we ended up having a few more guests as well. When John and I stepped outside after the service, 40 of our closest friends were waiting for us, waving pom poms and shouting their congratulations. An unconventional send-off, but it was the best gift I could have been given.

Like most other gifts in my life, I owe this one to Auntie Linda. After I had thrown my invitations in that bin, she had fished them out and together with my friend Natalie contacted each of the guests whose names were on those envelopes, inviting them to come and wave to us on our big day. I was totally surprised and, once again, grateful to have a family who loved me.

I was a married woman, and the wedding day had been perfect, pandemic and all. But so many people hadn't been able to join us because of COVID. Nothing that bad could last forever, I thought, and people would need something to celebrate when it was over. Why not celebrate my wedding—again?

We set the date for June 12, 2021, and our vendors graciously pushed everything back. This time, I did have my outdoor wedding, complete with dancing and more than eight guests. I picked a backdrop that featured the large gazebo in the film *Dirty Dancing*, one of my mom's favorite movies.

But of course, another calamity struck. The sky absolutely poured rain on the big day. The entire week before, my wedding planner kept checking the weather and sketching out a backup plan, and I said I would be prepared for any scenario. Besides, I was already married, so why stress?

But, inevitably, the rain did dampen my spirits as I sat in the venue surrounded by my family and closest friends, getting my hair and makeup done. I was so disappointed because it looked like, yet again, something beyond my control was going to ruin the well-thought-out plans I had envisioned. Needing a minute, I excused myself to the bathroom. I stood firmly with both feet on the ground and stared right into the mirror. *God*, I prayed, *please bring me back to this moment. Let me be immersed in every emotion. Don't let me miss the experience because of the weather.*

God answered my prayer. Right then, I was set free to enjoy a glorious day—rain or no rain. I admit to feeling relieved, though, when the rain stopped the very second my hair and makeup were done. One of my closest high school friends, Mary Stafford, took our pictures in the fields under heavy gray skies before the ceremony, and she had just snapped the last photo of John and me when the rain started up again. It poured for 30 minutes and then abruptly stopped.

Overjoyed at the change, I ran outside. People are not supposed to see the bride before the ceremony on her wedding day, but there I stood on the front porch, in my wedding dress, waving to people I hadn't seen in decades. I was just so excited!

Guests carried umbrellas to the venue and waited. Before I knew it, it was time for John to walk me to the altar. We made our way down the aisle toward my cousins, Justin and Jonathan, our officiants. Just as we made it to the altar and John took my hands, the sun broke through the clouds. Umbrellas went under the chairs, and the wedding began.

It was, in a word, glorious—a true celebration of love and life but without the same stress we might have felt had it been our first wedding.

Only later did I think about what I'd said when I sobbed in Aunt Linda's arms on the day my parents died. *Nobody will ever love me or want to marry me because I don't have parents.* Now I understand that my words were a teenager's attempt to comprehend the overwhelming loss of love that I felt that day. How ironic, though, that instead of never getting married, I got a wonderful husband and *two* picture-perfect wedding days.

As the Bible says, God really does give you more than you could ask for or even imagine (Eph. 3:20).

Pastor Layne Schranz officiated our
first wedding at Highlands Chapel
on May 30, 2020.
(Photo by David Lundgren)

Head over heels at our second wedding at
Mountain Lake Lodge in Pembroke,
Virginia, on June 12, 2021
(Photo by Mary Stafford)

Reuniting with my Rutgers gymnastics family in 2021
(Back row: Dawn Giel, Chrystal Chollet-Norton,
Kathy Galli, me, Bill Giel, Prudy Giel, and Dayna Giel.
Front row: Caitlin McKeever, Gina Roselle, Kelly Straka, Laura Iepson)
(Photo by Mary Stafford)

32

Cue the Confetti!

NOTHING—ABSOLUTELY NOTHING—MAKES ME FEEL THE SAME way as standing on a football field when the confetti rains down after a game. It reminds me of the layers of stories that fall around me every day.

Even though I was no longer an athlete winning championships, my story still grew to make an impact on others. In Springville, Alabama, I spoke at a Celebrate Recovery event. At first, I had a less-than-ideal mindset. I created labels for myself and had apprehensions about what stereotypes this group might be projecting onto me.

However, my worries vanished the minute I was introduced. I got more cheers of "Roll Tide" and "War Eagle" than I've ever gotten, even at a sports event. When I finished telling my story and my parents' stories, a few "Amens" got dropped in there, too. These people were passionate and competitive, my kind of people.

After the evening concluded, the line to meet and chat with me wrapped around the room. I was so encouraged by people's responses. One woman said, "As you shared your story and message, I felt like you were staring right at me. It was like you looked into my eyes and saw a reflection of who I was and what I went through." Best of all, she suddenly realized she wasn't alone and that she could find her way to the other side of her own pain and trauma.

Her kind comment stuck with me. I shouldn't have been surprised when, several months later as I was ordering a burrito at a Moe's in downtown Birmingham, the young man building my burrito looked at me like he knew me. "Hey, are you Lauren Sisler?"

At first, I thought he had seen me on TV, but then he said, "You spoke to us at Celebrate Recovery. Your message was powerful and really inspired me. That night, I actually received my one-month sobriety chip."

I was in the room when those chips were presented, and I remember this young man receiving his chip and seeing the sheer joy of accomplishment on his face as he was called up to accept it. I had, of course, cried right along with everyone else when he got the chip. Now, months later, here we were, reconnecting over a Moe's burrito.

"How are you doing now?" I asked him.

"I'm still sober. I have a steady job and a place to live. I'm standing on my own two feet again."

Once again, I was reminded of the power of one person's story.

Just after my (first) wedding, I covered a game between Arkansas and a big SEC rival.

At halftime, we usually do an interview with the leading coach. Arkansas' opponent was leading at the half, and their coach came running off the field. He was ready to get my interview done and over with so he could get in the locker room. He kept signaling with his hands, cueing me to hurry up. Of course, I couldn't do much until my producer gave me the green light. We finally did the interview, but I was left feeling flustered.

As halftime wound down, I caught the trailing coach coming out of the locker room—first-year Arkansas head coach Sam Pittman. He looked calm as if he had all the time in the world. I asked him a couple of questions, and he surprised me with his thoughtful and patient responses. I thanked him for his time and turned to walk away.

Then, I heard my name.

"Lauren!"

I turned around and glanced at the clock. It was ticking down, and it was just 1:49 until the second half kicked off, but still, Coach Pittman was heading toward me. When he caught up, he said, "You are really awesome at what you do. I mean that."

I was blown away! In less than two minutes, this man had to return to the field and help his team win a game that they were currently losing, and he was taking the time to tell a sideline reporter that she was awesome? That never happens!

The next week, I messaged him on Twitter to thank him for his kindness. He sent back a word of wisdom. "Lauren, it doesn't take long to let someone know you appreciate them and that they are impressive at their job."

In all my experiences and dealings with coaches on the sidelines, nothing has impacted me more deeply than that. I'll never forget the sense of gratitude I felt. Coach Pittman handed me a small gift that I have now shared with so many others. Thousands and thousands of people have heard that story and have realized that they, too, can plant the seed of gratitude in someone else's life.

Plant a seed, water it, and watch it grow! You just never know how your story and gratitude might touch someone else's life, even if it's years down the road—a truth I was about to witness for myself.

During a football game when the announcer in the booth tosses it down to me for a report from the sidelines, I typically have just 30 seconds to tell a story. Not much time, right? Well, let me tell you those 30 seconds can hold a lot of power.

In week four of the 2021 season, I was covering the Kentucky Wildcats playing the South Carolina Gamecocks when I met J.J. Weaver, a young outside linebacker for Kentucky who was born with six fingers on one hand. J.J. stands six feet five inches and tips the scales at 244 pounds, so it's hard for him to hide, but for two decades, J.J. did his best to hide his hand.

In grade school, his classmates called him an alien because of his fingers. The bullying even got so bad that J.J. would stuff two fingers into one finger of his glove when he was playing football so that his hand was less noticeable. He didn't care how much it hurt as long as he could protect himself.

Finally, in his sophomore season at Kentucky, J.J. felt ready to come out of hiding. He decided to step out of his fear and courageously tell his story, allowing me to share it on live television. During game week, I spent about 10 minutes on the phone with him, asking questions and gathering the details I needed for a 30-second report during the game broadcast. When the time came for me to share that report, I told everyone that J.J. was embracing his six fingers and that they actually helped him catch and grip the ball better.

Still, when my time was up, I felt a bit disappointed that I didn't get to tell more of his story. I had to leave out so many important details because of time! But in the end, 30 seconds was all we needed to make an immeasurable impact.

Shortly after the game, Kaye Cambron, a third-grade teacher from a local elementary school, emailed the Kentucky athletic department. She'd heard J.J.'s story on the ESPN broadcast, and Kaye, like J.J., had been born with extra fingers, six total on each hand. Unbelievably, two of Kaye's students were also born with extra fingers.

After seeing that email, J.J. decided to visit the teacher and the class. He shared his story and let all the kids try on his helmet, but he especially focused on the boy and girl born with extra fingers. He told them to embrace their uniqueness and the chance to be special. It's okay to be different, he said.

ESPN captured J.J.'s visit to that third-grade class, and millions of people viewed it. Best of all, the trajectory of those students' lives might have been positively impacted forever.

That's what can happen when you let go of your shame and fall in love with your story.

Kentucky linebacker J.J. Weaver shows off his six fingers.
(Photo by Elliott Hess/University of Kentucky Athletics)

Arkansas football coach Sam Pittman taught me a life lesson about gratitude.

33

That Little Girl with All the Trophies Actually Made It

IN SEPTEMBER OF 2021, I WENT BACK TO GILES HIGH SCHOOL FOR the first time in 19 years. Many people run away from their high school memories, but I felt like I had come home again. So many memories came flooding back as I walked the halls, even seeing a few teachers who remembered me. I was invited to speak to the entire student body of 8th through 12th graders.

I told them how I had loved jumping on the beds and the furniture as a toddler, so my parents enrolled me in gymnastics where I could burn off all that energy more safely. The coaches let me play in the foam pit for one week before they saw my potential.

I spoke about the years and years of hard work I'd invested in my sport, the injuries, the victories, the mistakes I'd made, and the trophies I'd won. I told them about going to Disney World even after I had fallen off the beam because life happens. We're going to fall down. But we have to get back up and keep moving forward. We can always find a way to celebrate, even when we feel the sharp pains of our disappointments and failures.

You can use your mistakes, failures, and disappointments as a catalyst for strength and resilience. No matter what happens, you can choose to build your life on a strong foundation. You will find open doors to the dreams that you never thought possible.

I shared with them about my career as a sports reporter and the long work days that turned into 3:00 a.m. trips through fast-food drive-thrus on the way home from football games. I told those students how I finally got my shot at ESPN.

But I also shared with them how things can go off script, and sometimes the best thing we can do is just to laugh at ourselves. "Guys, never be afraid to turn your would-be highlights into a blooper reel!"

Then, standing in front of hundreds of my hometown's teenagers, I got to the heart of my message.

For years, I was only willing to share part of my story—the part where I got back up and kept moving forward. On the outside, I had it all figured out. I was bubbly and energetic, the first one on the dance floor and the last one to leave. I was a fighter. I was an overcomer. I was the girl people looked up to because of the tragedy I had endured and the life of success I had found in my career as a sports broadcaster. I had it all together. At least, that's how it appeared, much like it had for my parents.

But, also like my parents, I had lived in denial on the inside. Like them, I had been trapped in the shadows of shame, and no matter how long I danced or how high I soared in my career, I had never felt free.

Deep inside, it was like I was feeding a toll booth with counterfeit money instead of authentic currency. I kept moving forward on that highway of life—in the sporty car with glossy wheels—but inside myself, I was a total wreck. At the root of my denial and shame lay a fear of judgment, so I was always striving for acceptance.

Finally, I could share with them the truth: I have been set free. No more shame. No more guilt. After ten years of hiding in the shadows, I realized that my parents were no different than me or anyone else. None of us is perfect, and none of us is exempt from life's difficult circumstances. It does not matter what side of town you grew up in, the car that's sitting out in that parking lot right now, your job title, or your income. None of those shiny, material things matter. What matters is how you choose to live.

We have the freedom to choose how we will respond to adversity. When tough times come—and, I told those teenagers, tough times come to everyone—will your resilience shine through?

What decisions will you make today that will influence the rest of your life? When I was 15, I made a promise to myself that I would never drink or do drugs. I would never chase a buzz or a high; I never wanted to lose control. I never wanted to morph into someone else for a short-term thrill. And, make no mistake, that thrill is only temporary—until it isn't.

One day, you wake up addicted, unable to stop, wishing like heck that you could, and now your entire world revolves around having that substance to get you through the day. Like water, food, rest, and shelter, that substance becomes a necessity; only instead of sustaining you, it will lead you down a dark path with no return.

There is no easy cure for addiction. It stays with you for the rest of your life, forcing you into a daily struggle. Freedom only comes when you admit you are powerless over your addiction and trust in a power greater than yourself to restore you to sanity.

And in closing, as I always do, I encouraged them—by all means, fall in love with your story, and find joy and gratitude in every single chapter of it.

When I finished, the entire student body rose to its feet and gave me a standing ovation. It was the most fulfilling applause I've ever received. Tears streamed down many kids' faces, and I knew the message had struck home.

Afterward, students crowded around me. One girl said, "I needed to hear that today. You have inspired me to keep moving forward." I found out later that she was the daughter of one of my classmates. Her comment and others like it gave me a deep sense of hope for the future.

As I was exiting through the auditorium doors, I passed by the trophy case. There was my photo! Alongside me was a picture of Marty Smith, another ESPN reporter who had graduated from our small high school. The school had even added an ESPN mic flag and a banner to the display to commemorate our success as sports reporters.

What I didn't know was that one of the students who left school that day was about to put the finishing touches on my story of overcoming shame.

Just after dinner that night in Virginia, my phone buzzed with a text message from Cora Ratcliffe Taylor, my longtime friend who had set up the speaking event at Giles. She had posted pictures of me and snippets from my speech on social media, and a response had come in.

Brady Thwaites, one of the students who had heard my talk at Giles, had gone home and shared my story with his dad, Eric.

"Son, I was there the day that story happened," Eric told Brady. "I was the deputy who investigated the scene."

Eric Thwaites, now an experienced narcotics investigator, remembered every detail of the night my parents died. Brady showed him the school's post with my picture on social media, and he read Cora's comments about the event. Then, he texted her.

> I saw your post about Lauren Sisler, and Brady told me about her presentation. I remember the day/night her parents died very well. Teddy Vaughn and I had just checked in on the daylight shift at 5 a.m. when we got the call from someone with the military who was on the phone with her father when he collapsed. I remember everything about it.
>
> I remember thinking how sad it was that she had to find her way back to NJ by herself with this burden. I remember the home and the pictures and her medals and awards. I remember thinking none of this scenario fits. I remember saying a prayer for her, and I had never known her until that moment.
>
> I'm glad to know she is doing well and is a success herself. I wish I had gotten the opportunity to meet her. There are always a few cases that never leave my mind. Hers is one of them.

When Cora forwarded the text to me, she added a note:

> I'm sure he'd love to connect with you. Typically when kids face something like you did they end up facing the same fate, and he was so thankful you didn't and you've been able to pull yourself out of it.

I was thunderstruck. So many questions buzzed in my head. Of course, I wanted to meet him! But I needed to be ready for that meeting. After taking a couple weeks to catch my breath and organize my thoughts, I wrote a three-page note to Eric Thwaites.

> Hi Eric,
>
> I want to first start by saying that this note comes to you with a heart full of gratitude. A couple of weeks ago when I came and spoke at Giles High School, I was overwhelmed with the emotions of being back home, standing on that stage in the auditorium, and even more so by the response I received from the students. They were incredibly grateful that I came and

spent the morning with them and opened my heart up to them by sharing my story.

What I didn't know is the good Lord put your son, Brady, in that auditorium until I later found out from Cora. She shared with me the text message you sent to her after Brady came home and mentioned I was there. Rarely am I speechless, but after reading that message, I was searching for words to capture the emotions I was feeling from your thoughtful and heartfelt account of that day, March 24, 2003.

We've never met in person, but somehow more than 18 years later, I feel connected to you through the experience you had that day that you mentioned has never left you. I have been hanging on to every word you shared with Cora in that text, from walking in the house and feeling that the scenario just didn't fit. You saw my medals and trophies and felt sadness for me as I had to find my way back home to this burden. And the prayer that you said for that young 18-year-old girl you had never met is profound. Lastly, what you said about most kids going through something like this and experiencing the same fate is often lost on me.

I often think that I didn't have a choice but to keep moving forward to find a positive outcome, but the reality and truth are I had plenty of choices and, like you, am so grateful I made the choices I did and had the love and support system around me to help me make those choices. It has been quite a journey, and I am so thankful to now have the opportunity and platform to share my story, and my parents' story, in hopes of helping others. And the story continues to grow.

Just last week I spoke at a 911 dispatchers conference and shared with them the message you sent to Cora, and the tremendous impact it has had on me in the few short weeks I've been sitting with it. Afterward, in receiving feedback, they felt so connected to that part of the story, which is amazing because it just reiterates the importance of sharing our stories and the power of connection.

God built a bridge between you and our family that day, and while the story for my parents ended tragically, I truly feel blessed by you. Thank you for your great service to our special community in Giles County. You and Teddy Vaughn will always have a special place in my heart. When I visit home again, I would love to swing by and meet you, not to recount the events of that day, but to say thank you.

Much love to you and your family, Eric.

God Bless!

Lauren

Eric's reply helped sharpen my thinking and further intrigued me about what he might be able to tell me about the night my parents died.

Lauren,

I must start by apologizing for not writing you back. I received your letter, and I admit it stirred a combination of memories and emotions, and I want you to know I sincerely appreciated your words. I still have the letter.

I have mentally scripted what I might say to you or how I should respond many times, but it's a bit of a struggle. It's hard to explain, and honestly, I don't talk about the things I have experienced over the last 26 years. I have only recently and rarely shared a few things with my wife out of the simple necessity of needing her to understand how some things that I've experienced come back to me and how it affects me at times. It was my goal from the start to be involved in as much as I could, and unfortunately, I have had to be involved in a tremendous amount of tragic situations.

Giles isn't as sleepy as most people think. Through all that time, I've always been cautious as to what I say to family who are caught up in something tragic and painful. I'm careful not as an attempt to hide anything but out of a desire to protect them from details that might cause more pain.

I realize this is a lengthy response, but I suppose I needed to explain why I haven't contacted you sooner and why my response has been so delayed. When I realized who you were that evening my son was telling me about hearing you speak,

it all came back. That's how these things work for me. Something reminds me, and it comes back in more detail than I
would prefer.

With that said, and I hope you don't think I'm crazy, lol,
I will talk to you and try and answer anything I can. I believe
you deserve that. When explaining myself, I sometimes do
better with the written rather than the spoken word. Hence
this long text. I suppose I needed to explain my hesitation, and
I hope you understand and accept my apology for not speaking sooner.

Eric Thwaites

Soon, we were making plans to meet in person. On April 28, 2022,
Aunt Linda and I drove back home to Giles County to meet Eric. Even
while I was getting ready that morning, I was full of emotions. By the time
I turned off the main road towards the sheriff's office, all those emotions
mixed together to form an overwhelming nervousness. My heart pounded
just the way it used to when I was about to compete in a gymnastics meet
and the same way it pounds now when I step onto the field to report on a
game.

I've interviewed the biggest names in sports, yet somehow this meeting conjured up more nerves than I've ever felt in my entire reporting career.

The old Lauren would have tried to shut down those feelings, but I
told myself to take in everything and allow myself to fully be where my
feet were planted. I expected it to be an emotional day, and it was!

Aunt Linda and I met Cora in the parking lot, and we walked to the
building together. When I reached Eric's office, he stood up, looked at me,
and said, "Can I hug you?"

"Of course, you can!"

We shared a long, meaningful embrace. Tears welled up in my eyes
right away, and I believe Eric got a little teary-eyed, too. We spent several
hours together that day. I met his mother, his wife, and even their new
puppy.

Before Auntie and I left town, we stopped at a little shop owned by
Mrs. Wheeler, the teacher who fundraised $3,000 to help Allen and me buy
back some of Mom and Dad's things at auction. I hadn't seen her since high

school, and I finally had the chance to give her my thanks in person with a hug.

Eric and I have continued to stay in touch, much like family now. He didn't know I had lost everything to the estate after my parents died. I knew very few of the details he shared with me about the night my parents died. I soaked up the information he provided. Later that day, he texted me and said,

> I want you to know I admire how you are and who you've become despite an unimaginable tragedy. I also want you to know how grateful I am that you are using your success as a platform for your story and message. It needs to be heard by so many people. And I guess I may have needed to hear it as much as anyone.

Our conversation didn't bring back my parents, but it was full of truth, and the truth always sets you free.

And that's what I am now—free. I'm no longer shackled by my trauma, my secrets, or my past. Yes, I lost the most precious people in my life, and until I get to heaven, nothing will undo that tragedy. But the love of my family and friends fills me with hope and joy. I have my husband, John, our precious baby boy, Mason, and our sweet yellow lab, Magnolia. I cherish each day.

I'm finally, deeply, and shamelessly in love—with my family, my life, and my story.

Shatterproof is the only way I ever want to live.

Back in the hallways of Giles High School for the first time in almost two decades to speak to the 8th through 12th grade students

Cora Ratcliffe Taylor and I share a passion for helping others find freedom from addiction.

A very special day meeting Deputy Eric Thwaites in April of 2022. This is a reminder that not all is dark in tragedy. My connection with Eric has brought a profound perspective and light into my life.

Thankful for the generosity of Mrs. Ann Wheeler and the Giles County community for helping my family in a time of need

Eternally grateful for the love and support of Aunt Linda and Uncle Mike

My wonderful husband John, beautiful son Mason, and our sweet Magnolia (Photos by Kristie Allen)

I will love you forever, Mason!

Afterword

*Even as a kid, I knew that when I grew up, I would be a mom
just like my mom. My future husband would be a dad just like
my dad. And our kids would never have to worry about anything because we would take care of them—just like my parents
always took care of me.*

A S I WAS PUTTING THE FINISHING TOUCHES ON THE MANU-
script that would become this book, this chronicle of what I learned
from my parents and what I learned about myself in the aftermath
of their deaths, I became a parent myself. On July 4, 2023, John Mason
Willard was born. Parts of my heart I didn't know existed burst alive that
day. I'd come full circle from being my dad's Little Lady Lauren to having
my own Little Man Mason.

It felt poetic that he was born on Independence Day when America
celebrates winning its freedom from British rule. After so many years, doc-
umented on these pages in often painful detail, of being locked in a prison
of denial about how my parents died, I had found my own freedom in the
truth. After too often thinking of myself as "less than" because I had lost
the patriarch and matriarch of my family, my husband and I assumed those
roles in our little family.

I wrote a lot on these pages about finding my identity as a child and
teenager in gymnastics, then how I found my professional sweet spot as a
sports journalist. What I know now is that as fulfilling as those things were,
and still are, I knew the instant I became a mom that it was my life's truest
calling.

I've made it pretty clear I have struggled to understand what led my
parents down the desperate road they traveled as they became addicted to

prescription drugs whose devastating power they didn't fully understand. But you know what? Becoming a parent myself has made me understand my mom and dad in a deeper, more profound way than I had imagined possible when my only relationship with them was as their child. Now we share a different bond—that of being parents. And as I fall in love anew every day with Mason, I feel a greater connection to Mom and Dad than I've ever known.

I understand the hopes and dreams they had for my future. The sacrifices they made to help me achieve the future I dreamed about. The pride that led them to beam at every accomplishment of mine, even those in my adolescent distractions that I dismissed as not that big a deal. I always knew, every day of my life, that I was blessed to have them, that Mom and Dad loved me. I want Mason to know the exact same thing. To experience the exact same things. To want to turn to me and John when life gets rough and he gets wobbly, the way I still want to turn to Mom and Dad. To fall in love with whatever his story turns out to be, the way I hope those who read mine will fall in love with theirs.

I pray Mason one day reads the quote at the beginning of this section, which also appears on page 26, and doesn't just understand more about his mom's life but feels the same way about his own life. That he draws inspiration and strength from the realization behind those words as I have.

I hope these words help him live a life, as his mother has been blessed to do, that is shatterproof.

—**Lauren Sisler**
July 24, 2023

Acknowledgments

AFTER SPENDING YEARS CONTEMPLATING IF I SHOULD WRITE A book, I finally did it. Yes, I finally did it! There was so much on my heart and so many things I wanted to share with others that couldn't possibly be covered in just one conversation. But then I kept asking if there was a "right time," and I found every excuse to keep putting it off. Maybe my story isn't that compelling. Maybe what I have to say isn't that meaningful or important. I realized though that the right time is "God's time," and I believe deep in my soul this book was meant for someone to read. Maybe it was meant for you, and I am so grateful this landed in your hands, and you made it to the end!

I also believe this book was meant for me to write. Through this process, I went on my own journey of seeking the truth and understanding my God-given purpose. I am amazed at how much I've learned and how much I've grown in these two years. My life has been enriched in a way I never imagined. I have so many people to thank and acknowledge as they paved the way for my life and the experiences that have led me down this path where I stand now.

First and foremost, glory be to God. My faith has continued to grow exponentially, and without Him, I wouldn't be standing at all.

To my parents, for your unconditional love and support. You brought me into this world and raised me the best way you knew how. And while 18 years with me here on earth seemed all too short, your presence in my life has continued to radiate through me and around me every single day since you went to heaven.

To my amazing husband, John, you are a special gift from God. Tested through years of patience, He finally revealed to me "the one." Despite my complexities, you demonstrate so much grace, giving me the freedom to just be me. I'm grateful for this life we share full of laughter, excitement, and joy. I am honored to be your wife and now the mother of our beautiful son, Mason, sharing in the blessings of being parents.

To my Little Man Mason, as I sit here, writing this with you snuggled up close against my chest, I feel my heart beating not only for me but for you.Filledwithundeniablejoy,I'mproudtobeyourmotherand, like your father, will love you forever.

To my brother, Allen, we have endured the peaks and valleys of this journey together. I light up when I think of the moments we shared with Mom and Dad. Despite our constant sibling rivalries, we have always remained a team. Team Sis forever!

To Auntie Linda, you were a presence in my life from the day I was born. You were Mom's best friend, never to let her down or leave her side. She looked up to her big sister, and so did I. While we never expected to experience a loss so deep, God ensured I didn't have to travel the unknown road alone. You stepped in with an unwavering love as if I was your own. You restored my hope in a bright future and lit my path every step of the way.

To Uncle Mike, the doctor and engineer, you've always kept things real. Calculated and intentional with every move, you led me in the direction where I had the best chance to prosper. Like Auntie, you weren't going to let me fail, but instead, you gave me the courage and confidence to succeed.

To my cousin Justin, you are like another brother to me. Seventeen trips to New Jersey to move me in and out of my dorm rooms and watch me compete in my gymnastics meets. Despite our family's great loss, you ensured I kept dancing through the storms.

To my cousin Jason, you were also like a brother to me and Allen. I love the memories we share of running the streets of Roanoke. I am also grateful that you brought your beautiful wife, Natalie, and sweet Lydia into our lives.

To my cousin Jonathan and his beautiful wife, Natasha, you all remind me every day to be proud of who I am and who I've become and that I am "Custom Made."

To Uncle Ross, I will always remember your preachings, especially overcoming fear with the protection of God, like in the Bible story of David and Goliath.

To Aunt Becky and my cousins Hannah, Benji, and Luke, the memories are fond and vast of our vacations together. I can still hear Mom and Dad's laughter when we all got together.

To my Grandma, Gramps, and MawMaw, you gave life to my mom and dad, teaching them how to raise Allen and me with an unconditional love only known to parents. Plus, you spoiled us, just as every grandparent does.

To my gymnastics coach Lisa Mason, you always encouraged me to push myself just a little harder so that I could say that I gave it my all. You would cheer me on and say, "Just do it, Lauren!" Those same words played out in my mind, over and over again, as I contemplated if I was equipped to write this book.

To my gymnastics coach Barb Jirka, I always watched in awe as you led a life of great faith. I still hold dear the booklet of inspirational quotes and scripture you gave your gymnasts one season before our state competition. I read each of those pages out loud with my parents sitting by my side over and over again through the years. I still have it and will always cherish it.

To my Rutgers gymnastics coach, Chrystal Chollet-Norton, like my other gymnastics coaches, you became another mom to me. More than anything, you gave me a chance to pick up the pieces of my life and patiently helped me put them back together again.

To my Rutgers gymnastics team trainer, Kathy Galli, you did so much more than keep my ailing gymnast body intact and in one piece. You were my life raft that kept me above water when I just wasn't sure I had it in me to keep swimming.

To Dawn and Dayna Giel, Laura Iepson, Kelly Straka, Gina Roselle, Caitlin McKeever (going with the maiden names from our glory days), and my Rutgers teammates, you have always embraced me for who I am, southern accent and all. You kept my spirits up during a time that I needed it most and never allowed me to quit on myself.

To my college roommate, Kara Spector, you are one-of-a-kind and somehow I was blessed enough to be paired with you. Coincidence? Not a chance. I am so grateful that the good Lord brought us together at Rutgers so that we could eventually swap titles from roommates to sisters.

To Kraig Feldman and Catie Mino, you two ensured the good times kept rolling through our four years together at Rutgers. The fun never stopped.

To my childhood friends and teammates Ellie Augustine, Amanda Patterson, Ashley Richardson, Mackenzie Payne, Kearstin Myers, Amanda Heptinstall, and Jenna Watson, you all were the first to show me the true meaning of friendship. We each shared a unique and special bond that I am forever grateful for.

To Mary Stafford, Joyelle Vinson, Trista Dooley, Chelsea Keating, Cora Ratcliffe, and my Giles County friends, you all welcomed me to our small town with open arms and showed me how to live my best life with no regrets.

To Deputy Eric Thwaites, the impact you have created in my life is significant and profound. You've given me insight that I was desperately searching for over the last 20 years. More than anything, you've shown me that all is not dark in tragedy. I'm so grateful our paths crossed in the most unsuspecting way. That's how we are reminded of life's greatest gifts that are only made possible by God.

To Mrs. Ann Wheeler for your incredible act of kindness, ensuring that Allen and I could hold onto some of Mom and Dad's most precious heirlooms and memories.

To April Blankenship for recounting the events of the tragic day that we lost my parents and for your determination to do everything in your power to bring them back to life.

To my in-laws BJ, Barry, Travis, and Elizabeth, I am grateful for your love and support and am honored to be a member of the Willard family.

To Timothy Alexander, you gave me permission to share my story. You always say, "It started with me." Well, my willingness to step out of my fears and truly embrace my story started with you.

To Natasha Ryan, Susan Bahorich, Lauren Weppler, Laura Goldman, Mike Stevens, Travis Wells, Grant Kittelson, Chris Miles, Jim Wharton, Laura Rutledge, Marty Smith, Paul Finebaum, and my TV family, you all saw my potential and gave me the confidence to keep chasing my dreams. And Jim Dunaway, I have you to thank for making Alabama my new home and the place where I am blessed to raise my family.

To my ESPN family, you are here alongside me, living the sports dream, and I'm so grateful for your love and support.

To Elle Hebel, thank you for discovering my sideline shimmy and helping me bring it to light!

To all the coaches and athletes whom I've been so fortunate to interview over the years, you helped me develop perspectives that have enriched my life in so many ways.

To my sports agent, Kristin LaFemina, for forging relationships and helping me "breakthrough" in my broadcasting career.

Acknowledgments

To my speaking manager, Christa Haberstock, for putting me on a stage where my voice is heard and my impact is magnified.

To Beverly and Randy McClendon for so gracefully taking on the role of being my "Birmingham parents." You are both such bright lights in my life. I am in awe of the way you've used your pain and heartache to restore hope in the lives of others.

To Mat and Kathy Whatley for investing your hearts in my mission to make a positive difference in the lives of others.

To Lucy and Frank Rush, when work kept me from being with my family on the holidays, you were quick to welcome me into yours.

To Sonja and John Richardson for being yet another reason why my home in Alabama is so near and dear to my heart. Because of you, I am often reminded of just how blessed I am to have such a great support system.

To Bill and Prudy for adopting me into the Giel family. I always knew I would have a place to call home just down the road from Rutgers.

To the Maloneys for sharing your home with me in Parkersburg as I was just beginning my journey in sports broadcasting.

To Audrey Trippe for helping me understand the complexities of addiction and serving as a source of hope, demonstrating that recovery and restoration are possible. I am so proud of you, girl!

To Danny and Haley Molloy, you showed me what it was like to be vulnerable and gave me the courage to find the truth in my story.

To my therapist, Neely Haynes, for helping me dig deep below the surface to find my true authentic self. Through our years of work together, I've learned to embrace the full spectrum of feelings and emotions that this life has to offer.

To Pastor Layne Schranz, Pastor Chris Hodges, John Maxwell, Mark Pettus, Kay Hargrave, and my Church of the Highlands family, you have brought great joy to my life and have ignited my passion for God and the work He has called me to do.

To the Kessingers for guiding my family's faith as we became part of the Oak View Christian Church and Spruce Run family.

To Holland Webb for dedicating your wordsmithing talents to this remarkable journey. These are more than just words on a page. Your gift of writing has given me peace and clarity, something I never thought I could obtain. I will forever be grateful to you (and to your sweet wife, Mandy) for committing your time and devoting your heart to this book.

To the High Bridge Books team, Darren Shearer, Kimberly Lippencott, and Sarah Berry, for believing in me and in the impact my story can have on the lives of others. Thank you for lending me your expertise to navigate this road to becoming an author. And Walt Taylor, thank you for seeing value in my story and steering me towards the resources to make this all happen.

To Gary Schneeberger for lending me your PR prowess to finalize and promote this book. I look forward to the road ahead as we put this book and its inspirational contents in the hands of many.

To my beta readers, Holli Hamner, Dean Dauphinais, Robyn Kown, Lindy Walker, and Katie Dunn for giving me an extra set of eyes and your trusted seal of approval.

To everyone whom I've ever had the honor of knowing—family, friends, and fans—for your boundless love and support. I'm endlessly grateful for the significant meaning and purpose you bring to my life. Much love and many blessings to you all!

Printed in the USA
CPSIA information can be obtained
at www.ICGtesting.com
JSHW070911060824
67621JS00002B/2